The Morality of Scarcity

The Morality of Scarcity

Limited Resources
and Social Policy

Edited by
WILLIAM M. FINNIN, JR.
GERALD ALONZO SMITH

Louisiana State University Press
BATON ROUGE AND LONDON

Design: Dwight Agner
Typeface: VIP Electra
Composition: The Composing Room of Michigan, Inc.
Printing: Thomson-Shore, Inc.
Binding: John H. Dekker & Sons, Inc.

"Morality and Foreign Policy" by John C. Bennett appeared in expanded form in *U.S. Foreign Policy and Christian Ethics* and is reprinted by permission from the September 14, 1977, issue of the *Christian Century*, copyright © 1977, Christian Century Foundation.
Excerpt from *The Night Is Dark and I Am Far from Home* by Jonathan Kozol, copyright © 1975 by Jonathan Kozol, reprinted by permission of the publisher, Houghton Mifflin Co.

Portions of "Distributive Justice and American Health Care" by Harmon L. Smith have appeared in somewhat different form as "Ethical Aspects of Medical Care for the Poor," in D. J. Self, ed., *Social Issues in Health Care*, copyright © 1977 by Old Dominion University Research Foundation, reprinted by permission.

Library of Congress Cataloging in Publication Data

Main entry under title:

The Morality of Scarcity.

The essays in this volume present the substance of formal lectures and informal seminars organized by the Project on Science and Social Policy at Louisiana State University, Baton Rouge, during the fall and spring semesters, 1976–1977
Includes bibliographical references and index.
1. Malthusianism—Addresses, essays, lectures. 2. Economic development—Addresses, essays, lectures. 3. Social ethics—Addresses, essays, lectures. 4. Social policy—Addresses, essays, lectures. I. Finnin, William M., 1946–   II. Smith, Gerald Alonzo, 1936–   III. Louisiana State University, Baton Rouge.
HB875.L49   330.1   78–21514
ISBN 0–8071–0485–X

To Ryan Patrick, David, and Daniel,
who will surely inherit the whirlwind

Contents

Preface and Acknowledgments

DURING the fall semester of 1976 and spring semester of
1977 at Louisiana State University, the Project on Science
and Social Policy brought to the Baton Rouge community a
series of distinguished scholars for serious discussion on a
range of topics related to ethical awareness and global interdependence. In formal lectures and informal seminars,
these representatives of the sciences, theology, social ethics,
and economics engaged members of the university, gov-
ernmental, business, and church communities in provoca-
tive reflection on the moral dimensions of social problems.
The essays in this volume present the substance of those
gatherings. It was my privilege and responsibility to direct
the project and to organize the occasions for these interactions.

The project relates to the larger community of Baton
Rouge served by The Uniting Campus Ministry at Louisiana State University. The Church's concern with the
quality of university and community life is neither surprising nor unprecedented, and it speaks creatively and boldly
about the concept of ministry and ethical responsibility
guiding the leaders of The Uniting Campus Ministry. The
creation of the Project on Science and Social Policy under
the organizational umbrella of the Church within the university addresses the university's often neglected responsibil-

ity of integrating ethics and technics, faith and practice, theory and organizational structure.

Funded by an Underwood Fellowship awarded by the Danforth Foundation of St. Louis, Missouri, the project fosters an atmosphere for dialogue among individuals whose professional and vocational responsibilities intersect each other and society but whose institutional insulation prevents sustained interaction. Two years and numerous events later, the Project on Science and Social Policy continues to assemble persons from disparate professional settings and disciplines. For related research, Herman E. Daly and Gerald Alonzo Smith received additional financial aid from the Rockefeller Brothers Fund.

The timeliness of the project is suggested by the enthusiastic support received from noted segments of the university and the nonacademic community. Several offices within the university provided matching financial resources for specific seminars and presentations. Among these we recognize with great appreciation the Louisiana State University Department of Economics and the Louisiana State University Student Union Academia Committee. We are also thankful to the Baton Rouge Humanities Group for its presentations.

To organize and implement a program of this nature requires the enthusiastic cooperation of many individuals committed to interdisciplinary exploration and ethical discourse. Chief among these persons is William H. Patrick, Jr., professor of marine science at Louisiana State University and faculty adviser to the Project on Science and Social Policy. Without his efforts and encouragement there would have been no project. Gerald A. Smith served as research associate for the project during its first year and serves as coeditor of this volume; no words can adequately describe his dedication. To the members of the board of directors of The Uniting Campus Ministry who risked with me the unknown during the planning of this project and to the student community at The Uniting Campus Ministry, I would like to express my genuine thanks for the support, criticism, and interest they have given to "the Danforth project" from its inception.

I am also grateful to the following persons: for his counsel, criticism, and encouragement in preparing this manuscript, Herman E. Daly, professor of economics at Louisiana State University; for reading and evaluating the manuscript in its early stages of preparation, Harold Sprout, professor emeritus of political science at Princeton University; for a detailed and sympathetic editorial evaluation of the final manuscript, Catherine Barton; for preparation of a neat typescript, Cathy MacMurdo; and all those from university, business, government, and church communities in Baton Rouge who gave of themselves during the project's first year. Many others, too numerous to identify, have contributed to this volume. Finally, a special thanks must be given Mary Bingham Finnin, my wife, for her enduring patience, loyal criticism, and joyful encouragement throughout our ministry together.

WILLIAM M. FINNIN, JR.

The Morality of Scarcity

Introduction

THEORETICAL systems are developed to help resolve the pressing questions that the world of experience presents to mankind. Thus the choice of a theoretical system useful in explaining the world ultimately depends upon the questions one considers most important or most pressing. For example, the orthodox social scientist, the neo-Marxist, and the neo-Malthusian would each perceive different sets of questions as most important. The fundamental ideal may be the same for all three ideological paradigms—how to achieve a better world for all. Yet, each theorist sees different immediate obstacles to his fundamental ideal and asks questions reflecting differing priorities. The orthodox social scientist, economist, or social planner studies problems of positive efficiency. The neo-Marxist investigates the social relationships and structural patterns of exploitation and power in society. The neo-Malthusian examines the effect of limited resources upon the quality of human life. Each tradition values different ends and seeks to diminish those things considered undesirable (relative inefficiencies given man's current desires constitutes the positivist's main object of attack, class exploitation the neo-Marxist's, and destruction of the environment through avoidable waste the neo-Malthusian's). These differing targets will in turn lead each to study different aspects of reality and consequently to formulate different methodologies and theories which will usually, but not always, reinforce the original values that led them to ask their particular question in the first place.

Each of these traditions contributes to the store of our knowledge. However, because the Malthusian tradition has been so long overlooked and because in recent history man has vastly increased his potential to destroy his environment, today one witnesses a renaissance of the Malthusian tradition. Since Rachel Carson sent shock waves through the pesticide industry with the publication of *Silent Spring* in 1962, a crescendo of literature has dealt with the inherent conflict between a finite environment and an ever-increasing demand on that environment by a growing industrialism and population.[1] The first articles and books following *Silent Spring* were argumentative and had as their aim the wakening of society from its complacent slumber regarding the destruction of its natural resource base. Though some of these earlier works were well documented and thoroughly researched (as indeed was *Silent Spring*), others were of a more popular and persuasive nature and evidenced more concern for the environment than for the facts of the case.

As more scholars became attracted by the controversy, they undertook more thorough studies. As a result of these inquiries, which came from many different disciplines, the first attempts at a synthesis were made. The *Limits to Growth* study is a significant and well-known step in this process.[2] Simultaneously, others were developing our conceptual knowledge of the problem. Kenneth Boulding's concept of the earth as a spaceship and Garrett Hardin's analogy of the environment as a "commons" focused

---

1. Because this is, in general, the same inherent conflict that concerned the Reverend Thomas Robert Malthus in 1797 in his essay on population, we have followed others and used the terms *Malthusian* and *neo-Malthusian* to label this concern over the degradation of the environment and exhaustion of global resources.

2. Sponsored by the Club of Rome, this study presents a comprehensive integrated index of global biophysical and economic constraints to development.

thought in a way that prodded many concerned scholars
to investigate the basic Malthusian conflict. Nicholas
Georgescu-Roegen's application of thermodynamics principles to economics developed formally a new theoretical
framework useful in ordering knowledge relevant to
Malthusian-type problems. *The Entropy Law and the Economic Process* is an excellent attempt to formulate explicitly
a more satisfactory theoretical paradigm.

Using these concepts and theories, tentative solutions
have been gradually derived, stating the appropriate steps
that individuals and society will have to take if these Malthusian problems are to be resolved. E. F. Schumacher, for
example, explored the implications of Malthusian constraints for the individual and suggested that individuals
needed a change in both goals and life-style. "Small is
beautiful" has become the watchword rather than "bigger is
better." Kenneth Boulding suggested that we consider
quotas for the number of children a family might have.
Herman E. Daly investigated what this limited resource
base meant for the industrialized and would-be industrialized societies of the world. Instead of an ever-growing
economy with an ever-increasing gross national product as
social and economic ideal, he proposed that societies opt for
a "steady-state economy" now and thus avoid its enforce-
ment later during a potentially catastrophic situation. But,
whether the solution calls for a change in the individual's
life-style or for a change in national strategy, all solutions
have as their aim the control of unwarranted expansion of
mankind's interference with the physical environment.
That environment ultimately supports everything man
does.

To the Malthusian all solutions will eventually require a
less wasteful, more rational use of our finite resources. This
requires a change in human behavior, both individual and
collective. Quickly, complex moral and humane questions arise. Such moral questions are integral to the neo-

Malthusian world view, as indeed they are of any world view. They should be faced honestly and openly; they will not simply vanish with the passing of time. Resolutions to such questions will require the understanding and expertise of individuals well versed in many of the branches of knowledge. The larger questions of social and biophysical survival involve constraints, population growth, society's use of resources, and the life-style of all of us. It can be easily shown that a complete analysis of moral questions in the neo-Malthusian paradigm requires the combined input of physicists, biologists, psychologists, demographers, engineers, agronomists, economists, sociologists, philosophers, and theologians, to identify several of the more obvious disciplines.

In this collection of essays the editors have attempted to shed some light on the moral dimensions of the neo-Malthusian problem and on the various solutions offered so far. As noted above, Kenneth Boulding, author of the opening essay, has played a large part in prodding the academic world into recognizing the Malthusian conflict through his timely essays dealing with the concept of "spaceship earth" and the finitude of our resources. He has written the foreword to the most recent edition of Malthus' first essay on population, and his concern for finding moral solutions to society's problems and his ability to do so are well known. In this essay, "Ethics of the Critique of Preferences," he takes a step beyond his previous essays in this field and analyzes the questions of values or preferences. He presents a spectrum of basic values in a categorization of basic value systems. He establishes a criterion for determining the desirability of basic value systems and thus investigates that topic so important to modern society and ordinarily avoided by the positivistic scientist—how to judge the basic values that ultimately motivate us as individuals and as societies. Boulding's essay takes up Harmon L. Smith's charge that "our moral crises derive from that ethical heteronomy; because we cannot agree upon the principles of virtue, we are in conflict about the practice of virtue."

Although Boulding eschews any elitism regarding what the "correct" values are, as in Platonic idealism, he nonetheless sets up a fundamental criterion of values which reflects the morality of reality. In other words, the morality that is conducive to lasting survival is desirable—basically an existential approach to the problem of values. In Boulding's vision, however, existence is generally benevolent, constructive, and evolutionary rather than malevolent, destructive, and dialectical. In this he departs from the dominant, despairing note of much twentieth-century existentialism.

In the second essay, "Heeding the Ancient Wisdom of *Primum Non Nocere*," Garrett Hardin builds upon his seminal work in the area of ecological ethics, or "lifeboat ethics." He issues an important and much-needed caveat to the would-be ethicist. The ethicist is usually sensitive to human sufferings and desires and has the best of intentions to alleviate them. When sufferings stem from poverty in the midst of affluence, the ethicist usually calls for a more equal distribution of the world's goods and services. Garrett Hardin cogently warns the ethicist to be sensitive not only to the sufferings of the current age; in typical Malthusian manner, he calls for an examination of the long-run implications of beneficent actions. It may well be possible that the temporary alleviation of current sufferings may cause permanent damage to the ecosphere by expanding a regional or global population beyond its carrying capacity, thus unintentionally augmenting total human misery.

In a carefully woven study, Herman Daly probes the relationship between fundamental moral values and scarcity of natural resources. He deftly shows not only that it is impossible to escape the moral problems flowing from having insufficient natural resources for lifting all the present and future world to an American standard of living, but that, even if it were possible, it would not be desirable. For Daly human social and economic development depends upon recognizing some external constraints. Such constraints force us to acknowledge our humanity and dependence and ultimately may force us to reform our interior selves, since we cannot recreate the exterior so as to eliminate all external limits. Without the acknowledgment of such constraints, man's *hubris* becomes unbounded. True culture and civilization can be found only in man's harmonious adjustment to the limits of nature, not in an unrealistic attempt to escape from such limits by simply employing a technological fix. Such a response ignores the reality of absolute limits.

In his discussion of the ethical implications of limits, Daly reminds us of the essence of human nature as it relates to creation. Man is a created creator. Some past ages of man have perhaps overemphasized the fact that man is created and have minimized his role to that of a passive acceptor of fate, but it is also possible to overemphasize man's creative ability and to perceive him as a god-like creator. Daly does more than identify this latter error; in a manner original for an economist, he directs us to a corrective.

The next essays deal with more particular aspects of the Malthusian problem. Drawing on his long experience as the agronomist who founded and directed the Rockefeller Foundation's International Rice Research Institute in the Philippines, Robert Chandler explores the realistic possibilities of increasing per capita food production. In the first half of "Some Thoughts on the Global Food and Population Problem," he brings us up-to-date on the problem that originally troubled Malthus, the possibility of mass starvation. He looks to the future and outlines a global strategy for avoiding famine. On one level, Chandler's conclusions seem to contradict those of Garrett Hardin's essay herein. On another level, these two essays complement one another. The biologist and the agronomist, though both life-science scholars, view biological life from different perspectives, and the difference shows in these essays.

Harmon Smith delves into medical ethics in an expanding and increasingly industrialized world economy. He asks whether this industrialization has brought forth a "growth-mania" affecting those skilled professionals (physicians, attorneys, educators, clerics) who ideally treat their clients not only professionally and scientifically but also personally and compassionately. Specifically, as health care becomes more complex and specialized, he wonders if the medical profession has responded to the challenge of continuing to deal with the individual *qua* individual, or if it has taken the easy way out and dealt with its patients in a mechanistic, isolated, and rigid manner.

John Bennett questions the significance of the interaction of economics, politics, and problems of justice for nationalism and the morality of nations. Since finitude of resources is ultimately a global problem, he asks, can nationalism deal with neo-Malthusian types of problems effectively and constructively?

In the concluding assay, Donald Shriver investigates briefly the role of business, academia, government, and the Church in a world that must deal with intertwined ecological problems. A social ethicist, he calls for solutions respecting the freedom, security, and unique creativity of each individual. In the face of global biophysical constraints triggered largely by modern civilization, he contends, we must recognize that individuals make up present and future societies.

The epilogue brings to light some of the forgotten followers of Malthus (or, if you prefer, predecessors of Rachel Carson) by providing a brief history of Malthusian thought from 1797 to 1962. Those years were characterized by almost unlimited industrial and resource-base expansion, and analyses of environmental degradation and resource exhaustion were considered to be of little value. Although predictions of impending catastrophe due to shortfalls of natural resources turned out to be premature, their authors deserve to be remembered for at least two reasons. First, representing another era and culture, they may demonstrate insights into the Malthusian problem we have overlooked. Second, the Malthusian is well aware that just as the future will be a product of the present, the present is a product of the past. Therefore, an understanding of the current state of the art in neo-Malthusian ethics and economics requires an understanding of what was written (and not written) in the past.

Ethics of the Critique of Preferences

KENNETH E. BOULDING

ECONOMICS bases a great deal of its analysis on the description of individual preferences. It has developed a fairly elaborate mathematical and graphical technique for doing this, through the description of a utility function that postulates an ordinal utility index. Thus, any description of the state A of an individual which is preferred to a state B will have a higher position on the utility scale. With this relatively simple device a surprising amount can be said about the general character of preferences. Every elementary textbook of economics will have a discussion of indifference curves by which these preferences are described. Economists tend to take preferences for granted, though there is not much description in the literature about how they are formed and learned. We know that they mostly *are* learned, for genetic preferences in human beings are very primitive. At a certain level of abstraction, of course, it is perfectly legitimate to take preferences for granted and to analyze the consequences of given preferences, even in the light of the fact that actual preferences are constantly shifting. Realistic theory of social dynamics must take the formation of preferences into account. It is perhaps Thorstein Veblen's major contribution to economics that he called attention to this fact, though possibly because of the coruscating brilliance of his language, economists have remained remarkably indifferent to his criticisms.

What might be called first-order ethics involves a critique of individual preferences. I am talking ethics when I say, "I think your preferences are miserable," or "splendid," as the case may be. Even that almost extinct species, the cultural relativist, is really talking ethics when he says, "I am not in a position to judge anybody's preferences." The statement that one set of preferences is as good as another is just as much an ethical statement as one which says that one set of preferences is better than another. We could even suppose that there is a second-order ethics which is a critique of first-order ethical systems. I might say, "I think your ethics is ill-founded" or, even more sharply, "I think your critique of my preferences is wrong." Theoretically, I suppose we could go to third order and an infinite regress, but we rarely go beyond the second order in anything in the real world, whatever we do in mathematics.

A critique of preferences is inevitably a critique of decisions, for preferences only become visible and significant at the point of decision. A decision indeed consists of arranging an agenda of projected images of the future in some rough order of preference and selecting the one at the top of the list. This is the economist's "theory of maximizing behavior," which simply says that everybody does what he thinks is best at the time, a proposition so hard to deny that it does not have very much content.

The critique of individual preferences and decisions takes a number of different forms. It may involve a critique of the identity of the preference maker or decision maker, particularly on the grounds that the identity and the agenda of decision and of preference is too narrow. A critique based on a low value given to selfishness would be an example. There is nothing in the theory of preference or decision which says that an individual cannot exhibit love, benevolence, a sense of community, an identification with a larger group, and so on. Individuals can also exhibit hatred, malevolence, and enmity. Technically, it is easy to include benevolence and malevolence into preference descriptions simply by including the individual's perception of the welfare of another person, or of a group or community, as a variable in his preference or utility function. If my perception of an increase in your welfare makes me feel better off, I am benevolent; if it makes me feel worse off, I am malevolent. Selfishness, in which I am unaffected by contemplation of another's welfare, is the knife edge between benevolence and malevolence and is actually very rare. Most people are at least either mildly benevolent or mildly malevolent. One ethical critique here is essentially that selfishness involves too narrow an identity, as in the proverb that a man wrapped up in himself is a very small parcel. And as identity is inevitably bound up with the community with which we identify, it leads into benevolence for that community and perhaps into malevolence towards others. The ethic of universal love is really an ethic of the second order. Most ethical systems fall short of this.

The critique of identity is perhaps a special case of a larger critique or set of critiques which perhaps can be collected under the general, if rather vague, term *health*. The very obvious case here is addictive preferences such as drugs, whereby continued satisfaction of the preference diminishes the utility to be derived from subsequent satisfactions. More things may fall into this category than is generally recognized, even perhaps education and riches!

There is another set of critiques which might fall under the general heading of irrationality; for instance, inconsistency in preferences, loving something today and hating it tomorrow. Self-deception is something that is certainly real though hard to define. It is related to our failure to listen or to receive feedback, and this can result in errors in our image of the possible choices and the values we place on them. There are critiques of some presumed standards of quality or aesthetics or elegance. For instance, in *The Joyless Economy* Tibor Scitovsky criticizes the preferences developed in market-type societies as having a low quality on a scale of aristocratic values.[1] There are tricky problems here. The rich have always criticized the morals of the poor and the poor the morals of the rich, and one certainly does not have to be a cultural relativist to see that there is some relativity in cultures and that all critiques are not consistent. It would be interesting to go through the seven deadly sins and to see them as a critique of unhealthy preferences: pride preventing learning and feedback, anger preventing cool and rational judgment, lust involving inordinate desire which destroys rational choice, envy involving malevolence at the welfare of another, greed or covetousness involving not only inordinate desire but lack of benevolence and a crippling of the identity, gluttony likewise involving a loss of restraint and rational choice, and sloth involving the decay of the decision-making power itself.

Agreement on these critiques is not easy to obtain and a possible approach that may produce greater agreement is to try to identify the more extreme cases of perverse dynamics. This is the situation in which the interaction of the decisions of different individuals leads to a dynamic in which all of them become worse off even in their own estimation. The famous "prisoner's dilemma" in game theory is a good example. We have the interaction of two decision makers, each of whom may be either good or bad. If each is good, then both are better off; if each is good, however, it may pay one to be bad; and then if one is bad, it pays the other to be bad. So they end up both being bad, in which case both are worse off. Arms races, quarrels, marital discord, labor disputes constantly provide us with examples of this perverse pattern. Essentially, it can only be avoided by a learning process that creates a sense of community and, therefore, imposes a taboo on temporary advantages that may result in long-run disadvantages.

1. Tibor Scitovsky, *The Joyless Economy: An Inquiry into Human Satisfaction and Consumer Dissatisfaction* (New York: Oxford University Press, 1976).

A similar case is what Garrett Hardin has called the "tragedy of the commons," in which it pays each individual to overuse a common resource to the eventual detriment of all. Here again, the answer lies in the development of community, for even the solution of dividing up the commons into individual properties rests on the existence of a community that will give each individual security in his property. Security in property depends on there being a taboo against interfering with it.

It is no accident that ethical systems have so often been concerned with taboo. A critique of preferences which, in effect, limits the agenda by removing potentially damaging choices is often highly practicable. The critique of preference that says you should put a zero preference on certain inadmissible items is much easier to understand and to observe than a critique that says you should put higher values on some items of the agenda and lower values on others.

A large area in which the critique of preferences may be valid though often very difficult, is in our preferences with regard to sizable systems—politics, legislation, ideologies. The analysis of ideological preferences is still in its infancy; but it is very much needed, for people's political preferences are often guided by much less knowledge of the agendas than are their preferences in personal matters. In general, the larger the system, the harder it is to develop correct images of it and the easier it is for our preferences to be based on an illusion of what we are really preferring. One suspects that a great deal of political controversy such as that between the radicals, liberals, and conservatives, is based on false images of the nature of the alternatives. Under these circumstances preferences will be based on imperfect samples or on aspects of systems which may be salient to the observer but not very important. A very large pathology of preferences becomes possible.

A critique of preferences is useless unless preferences can be changed as a result of the critique. This, of course, assumes that preferences are learned and not given from genetic structure or other physiological, uncontrollable properties of the nervous system. There is no doubt that preferences are learned and that they are malleable in response to criticism. Nevertheless, there are limits to the learning process, and the problem of how to make criticism effective within the learning process is far from being solved. An understanding of the limits of this learning process, therefore, is important in second-order ethics, because an ethic which assumes that these limits are either much wider or narrower than they turn out to be will be unrealistic and itself must come under criticism.

Some limitations are placed on the learning process by the genetic structures and biological inheritance of the individual, even though for most people in the "normal" range these do not seem to be very important. However, we certainly cannot blame a tone-deaf person for being insensitive to the glories of great music, nor can we expect a color-blind person to be highly sensitive to the virtues of great painting. Whether there are genetic deficiencies in moral sensibilities we really do not know. The evidence for impact of double chromosomes seems dubious, but so little is known about overall genetic determinants of human growing and learning, one would hesitate to say that no genetic components of moral sensitivity exist. We are pretty sure, however, that if these exist, they are very subtle and do not correspond to anything we could call race or class.

Another very large problem is the complex interaction between our images of fact—what we think the real world outside us is like—and our images of value and preferences. They mutually interact. Our preferences and value structures operate as filters in determining our perceptions of fact. It is well known in psychiatry that we filter out the unpleasant and the unacceptable and that this frequently makes our image of the world unrealistic. The other side of the coin is that false or incomplete images of reality have a very profound effect on our values and preferences. Simple faith may be better than Norman blood, but it often does not survive higher education. Dialectical views of the world, for example, produce a great deal more legitimated malevolence than do evolutionary views. On a smaller scale, our perceptions of what is possible and what is not, that is, of the possibility boundaries surrounding each individual, also have effects on our preferences. There is what I have called the "sour grapes effect"—what we can't get we decide we don't want. One of the interesting problems in this regard is the failure to recognize tradeoffs. We all have a strong tendency to want to have our cake and eat it too. Hence, we are inclined to deny that tradeoffs exist and to make judgments solely on the grounds of our evaluation of one element in the real world. Such judgments do not take into account related elements which may alter with a change in the first element on which we are concentrating. Prohibition was probably a good example of an ethical critique which failed to recognize certain tradeoffs and perhaps ended up doing more harm than good. The current move for the prohibition of nuclear power could easily fall into the same trap. People are apt to think that because they have demonstrated that something is bad, they have also demonstrated that it should be abolished. Merely demonstrating that something is bad, however, never proves that the alternative might not be worse.

Another problem in the critique of preferences and in its effects relates to the effectiveness of persuasion. An ethical critique is essentially a persuasive fact. Some means of persuasion, however, are much more powerful than others, and there is no necessary correlation between the effectiveness of a persuader and the rightness of what he is advocating. This gets to be a particularly difficult problem if there is a monopoly of persuasion in society, as in Catholic Spain in the Middle Ages, or in Mao's China. Here the power of persuasion may be very loosely related to the truth of the message. One has an uneasy feeling indeed that there are situations in which this relation is negative, that it is easier to persuade people of nonsense than of the truth.

Nevertheless, one does fall back on the great principle of Abraham Lincoln—you can't fool all of the people all of the time. Happily, a certain asymmetry exists between truth and lies and between truth and error, because both lies and error can be found out but truth cannot. One hopes that the real world is ultimately the greatest persuader of all and that whatever the aberrations along the way, there is a long drive towards reality in our image of the world and also in our preferences and values. This raises the complex question of whether there is something that could be called "truth" in preferences and valuations, as there is in our image of fact. The cultural relativist would seem to deny this. But I do not see how the process of learning preferences and values can be understood without a presumption of some kind of asymmetry between the better and the worse, the truer and the less true. There may not be an absolute single truth in matters of value, but there surely is error. The truth may be an area rather than a point, but there is a difference between being inside it and being outside it. Values are neither random nor arbitrary, though they may be diverse; therefore, the critique of error in them is a highly necessary human activity.

The mere observation of the existence of ethics as a social phenomenon does not in itself constitute a critique of ethical systems. Critique does imply that there is a truth in ethical systems which in some sense is asymmetric with error. The search for this truth, however, is a long process of traveling hopefully rather than arriving. We are a long way from a universally accepted image of ethical truth. Nevertheless, the search for this holy grail is not meaningless. There are, at least, considerations that warn us when we are off the track.

Any second-order ethic that evaluates existing ethical systems must involve a reasonably clear image of the processes through time by which the relevant state of the world changes. What is relevant depends on the nature of the ethical system itself, particularly the one that is most valuable in the eyes of the critic. A useful criterion, at least to start with, is that most things affected by human behavior are relevant in the state of the world. Thus, if human behavior results in some other species becoming extinct or in the landscape becoming changed, these things are relevant in the ethical evaluation. The state and condition of the earth's human population, past, present, and future, is clearly relevant. Things unaffected by human action, such as the condition of the sun or the earth's core, can be neglected in ethical appraisals. Changes in these things, though, may alter the conditions of the relevance of the universe and may, therefore, have to be taken into account. A natural catastrophe like an ice age would profoundly change the ethical problems that the human race has to face.

Having defined the relevant universe, the next task is to understand the dynamic processes by which it changes, particularly the impact of human decisions upon it. One can identify two large processes in the dynamics of the universe which are significant to the ethically relevant part of it. The first is the process of ecological interaction and evolution. In this model we divide the universe into the three main kinds of species: physical species such as compounds, crystals, rocks; biological species; and social species, which consist of human artifacts. There are material artifacts like automobiles or hybrid corn, and organizational artifacts like a tribe, nation, church, business, corporation or foundation. Finally there are persons, produced partly as a result of the genetic information in the fertilized egg from which they began, but also produced by the enormous flood of information that both reaches them through the senses and is generated internally in the imagination and in the mind.

The definition of a species is often difficult and sometimes has to be a little arbitrary. Most species consist of a set of reasonably identical members, and if the members differ there is always a question as to which individuals should be included and which should be excluded. This problem is more difficult in social species. The genetics of the species are extremely complex and may involve the whole knowledge stock of the society. Biological species can be defined fairly easily by the genetic rule: An organism is not a member of a given species if it cannot contribute to the gene pool of the species in producing further members. With social species, definition is more difficult, and we have to make judgments as to what constitutes a reasonably homogeneous aggregate. Thus, is the three-wheeled vehicle an automobile? Is a hospital a business? Are the Palestinians a nation? Are Quakers Protestants? Difficulties, however, tend to occur at the margins and do not affect the fundamental validity of the model.

The evolutionary model then supposes that each species increases in numbers if its additions (births) exceed its subtractions (deaths) and declines if subtractions exceed additions. If a species declines long enough it will become extinct. The additions and subtractions are functions partly of the size of the species itself but also of the size of other species in its significant environment. It is this interaction of species that constitutes selection. Much confusion has been caused by the unfortunate metaphors Darwin used in describing the process. The survival of the fittest is almost meaningless, as fitness simply means fitness to survive. The critical process here is that a species will survive if it finds a niche, that is, if its environment is such that there is some population level at which it will neither grow nor decline. Similarly, "struggle for existence" is an inapt metaphor, because struggle is quite rare, especially in the biosphere, and is much less common than most people think in social systems. It is significant in so far as it affects the size of the niche of a given species, and this depends on many other things besides struggle.

A system of interacting species may move toward an ecological equilibrium, but the equilibrium is continually disturbed by mutations, that is, genetic, physical, or social changes in the parameters of the system. Any mutation alters the niches of all the interacting species in an ecosystem. Some may then move toward extinction, while new niches may be created into which new species may grow. There is nothing in the concept of evolution to say that it has to have a direction in time. Yet, from the record of the past—rocks, documents, and surviving artifacts—we do deduce that there has been a direction towards something with which we identify but cannot easily define. It might be called complexity, intelligence, power, or divinity. We are strongly conscious of some direction that is up rather than down.

The general evolutionary process is affected, especially in social systems, by a second, more direct pattern of interaction involving struggle, conflict, fighting, winning, and losing. These are the dialectical processes. They are quite rare in biological evolution but have some significance, the size of which is difficult to estimate, in social systems and in the course of human history. The fact that I am speaking English in a town with a French name suggests that a French-speaking system at first won and then later lost. The content of what I am saying, however, does not depend very much on the language I happen to be using. One suspects, therefore, that the more peripheral things like language or superficial aspects of culture are determined by these dialectical processes. Even in social systems the large changes may be essentially ecological and take place through the complexity of ecological interaction and mutation in the form of new ideas, new technology, new inventions. Dialectical processes are the waves on the great river of history. For those whose canoe may be engulfed in them, they are very important; for understanding the main direction, they are much less important. This does rule out the possibility that the waves might sometimes be large enough to break through the banks and create a whole new course for the river. This phenomenon, one expects, is very rare.

In the light of the model presented above, ethical systems are seen as a type of social species, coexisting with the aggregate of interacting social species. In a social ecosystem there is a close symbiotic relation between ethical ideas and the particular cultures and subcultures within the larger society. A culture or subculture could almost be described as a set of human beings defined by the common attribute of an ethical system. Within a particular culture the critique of personal preferences by the cultural values is very strong, and individuals who do not conform either exclude themselves from the culture by migration, or are excluded through exile, prison, or even death. The growth or decline of ethical structures is very closely bound up with the growth or decline of the cultures in which they are embodied. One of the critical problems, which unfortunately is not easy to solve, is that of the role of the ethical system of a culture in its growth or decline, success or extinction. The ethical system is not the only factor that determines the future, success, or failure of a culture, although it is undoubtedly an important factor. This means that the spread or contraction of different ethical systems around the world depends in part on the nature of the ethical systems themselves; but it depends also on events and phenomena which are somewhat independent of these systems and may range from climatic changes to technical changes in transportation, food production, medicine, or weaponry.

The geography of cultural interaction is also very important. The expansion of a technologically vigorous culture may be halted when it meets an equally vigorous one but may be relatively unimpeded when it meets less technologically advanced cultures. Thus, the spread of European cultures and their attendant value systems to the Americas was perhaps more related to fifteenth-century improvements in European sea transportation and the fact that the indigenous American cultures did not have either gunpowder or the wheel, than it was to any ethical superiority of the European cultures. The spread of European cultures through Asia during the same period was severely impeded by the fact that beyond the coasts Asian cultures were much better organized and more technically developed than the North Americans.

In spite of all the extraneous factors, there can be little doubt that the nature of the ethical system of a culture does have non-random long-run effects on its chances of expansion or survival. It is not merely through the accident of technology that we find the Ten Commandments, which originated in a small tribe in the Middle East some three thousand years ago, have spread around the earth from Patagonia to Honolulu. Nor is it surprising that the golden rule in one form or another is found in virtually all the great world religions. An ethic of total personal selfishness and aggrandizement is bound to be destructive to a culture, and ethical systems that achieve a good balance between the individual and the community are likely to create cultures that prosper. It is not surprising that nearly all surviving cultures give a strong ethical emphasis to the virtues of family life and the nurture of children. Population increases only when births exceed deaths. On the other hand, cultures like the Mayans, which are too successful in creating population increase, may run into overshoot and Malthusian collapse. An ethic of moderation in the use of resources, perhaps through some sort of taboo, may also have a place in long-run survival.

In times of rapid social and technical change the necessity for second-order ethics and the critique of existing ethical systems becomes much more urgent. During such times, of which the present is a good example, one feels the need for a third-order ethic, the critique of critiques, simply because the existing critiques often seem to be made in the absence of widespread understanding of their possible consequences. In the twentieth century, for instance, we have seen a very strong critique of ethical systems that justified inequality and discrimination. This has something to do with the technological change in transportation and communications, which has permitted a far greater volume of information to be generated around a society than in any previous period and has resulted in the political mobilization of previously passive segments of society. Under these circumstances a critique of existing ethical systems in the direction of finding new ethical systems to handle the situation more effectively is a high priority. But this "mobilization ethic," as it might be called, is itself subject to severe pathologies. In the form of Marxism it has produced dull, tyrannical societies that have slowed down the pace of social evolution, have failed to liberate the human spirit, and have achieved mobilization only by a monopoly of information through its inevitable bureaucratic corruption. South Africa is a good example of a society in which ethical critique has failed both to develop a more integrated society and to solve problems of integration in a society of such extraordinary cultural heterogeneity.

At present, a desperate need is felt for third-order ethics directed at evaluating the conventional liberal wisdom, and still more the conventional socialist wisdom, of the second-order ethical critiques. This task, however, requires not only a large commitment to improving the understanding of the actual dynamics of social systems but also an understanding of the metaphors and the "language magic" that will make these interpretations plausible and understood. One has a depressing feeling sometimes that, just as it is impossible to create a new religion by thinking and acting deliberately, so it may be virtually impossible to create a genuinely third-order ethic, which like religion may have to wait upon the luck of relevation. But whether such luck is real randomness or simply an order unknown to the human mind is a deep question I gladly leave to others.

Heeding the Ancient Wisdom of *Primum Non Nocere*

GARRETT HARDIN

SUCCESSFUL politicians and salesmen follow an invariable rule—never explain, never complain—and thus attempt to keep doubt from entering the minds of those they would convince. Scientists and scholars who venture into the public arena cannot always follow this simple rule, not if they want to keep their good name as seekers of the truth. One *does* make mistakes, after all. Defending a mistake uses up time and energy that are better devoted to approaching the truth.

My position is essentially this: I want to encourage a critical examination of how we interact with poor people. To be accurate, we should not speak of foreign aid but of foreign intervention, for we do not know, without a critical investigation, whether our intervention is aiding. Naturally, we hope that it is, but let us not use the prejudicial term foreign *aid*. By habitually using the word *intervention* we can keep our minds alert to the very real possibility that we may be harming the recipients of our attentions.

Let's review some of the facts. On the technological level we know that many of our interventions in the past have been disastrous. A well-known example of an unsuccessful intervention involved the High Aswan Dam in Egypt. Initially, the United States was scheduled to build it; but we had a political falling-out with Gamal Abdel Nasser, and, as a result, we withdrew from the project. Russia took over and built a dam, fortunate for the United States, because it has been a disaster for Egypt.

The dam was built to impound water, which would be used to irrigate millions of acres and to generate hydroelectric power. The project looked innocent enough, but even before the dam was built, a few voices cried havoc. These voices were principally those of ecologists, whose warnings were rarely heeded back in the early 1950s. One of the things they pointed out was that with the completion of the dam the water going down the Nile would be completely controlled and there would be no more yearly floods. Every year the water had spread over large areas of land and, in the process, accomplished two things. First, it left behind it a thin layer, about one mm. thick, of very rich soil that fertilized the land. Second, the flooding washed away salts that had accumulated in the irrigated soil between floods. This system worked so beautifully that for six thousand years agriculture in the Nile Valley operated at a high level of productivity. At no other place in the world has agriculture continued for so long without exhausting the land.

Once the dam was finished only a small amount of water could go down the river. Irrigation of dry land is always, in the long run, destructive to the soil, because as the water evaporates, its salts are left behind. Each year the salt accumulates until the land reaches a point that makes agriculture impossible. This has happened in the Tigris-Euphrates Valley. There are ways to unsalt the soil, but they are very expensive in terms of time and effort. The simplest way requires a lot of water, which of course, is just what an irrigation economy is short of. Because ecologists were ignored, an ancient agriculture is destined to be destroyed.

Also, biologists ineffectively warned about the increase of disease that would be caused by the dam. Schistosomiasis is a serious parasitic worm disease in the Nile Valley. The ideal condition for the parasite is a lot of standing water. Year-round irrigation creates standing water. The ravages of schistosomiasis have increased since the dam was built, but Egypt does not have money for the necessary medical treatments.

In addition the dam caused damage that was not foreseen, as far as I know. The Nile in flood previously carried a load of silt into the Mediterranean, which furnished the nutrients for the food chain supporting the sardines in the eastern Mediterranean. This industry is now 95 percent ruined, and it will never come back. Another consequence of the dam is the loss of fertile land in the delta, in which the Nile floods had deposited silt against the steadily erosive forces of the Mediterranean. The Mediterranean is now gaining on the delta, and Egypt is losing thousands of acres of delta land each year. Ultimately, the entire delta will go. These losses must be balanced against the gains of irrigated land in the upper region of the Nile; however, it is clear that Egypt loses.

When the dam was first planned, demographers predicted that the growth of the Egyptian population during the time of construction would absorb any gains in productivity created by the dam. The prediction has proved true, and Egypt is now falling behind. The nation is no better off now than she was in the beginning, and her situation will become worse. The evidence is in the daily newspapers. In January, 1977, there were riots in Cairo because President Sadat, having looked at economic facts, said that he would have to let the price of food rise. The United States, which for political reasons wants stability in that region of the world, then provided loans of money and food. Sadat reversed his decision, and the price of food was lowered to its previous level.

No one has confronted the idea of population control for Egypt; moving from one crisis to another, politicians have just bought time. The United States is not the only country that finances this evasion. We give about a billion dollars a year to Egypt, and the Arab countries give about three billion. Egypt's economy is propped up on borrowed crutches, and there is no effective attack on the fundamental problem, which is simply too many people on too little land. The only solution is to stop population growth; ultimately Egypt must actually reduce the size of her population. All other approaches are makeshift.

The Aswan Dam is only one of the many mistakes the developed world has made in trying to help poor countries. The United States generally avoids tackling organizational problems within recipient countries for a good reason. We are usually interested in political stability and, therefore, direct our interventions through existing governments without questioning whether it is the best government for the people. There is no way to get aid directly to the people. We could make gifts to revolutionaries; but this would be a dangerous course to follow, because we do not know which revolutionaries have the best ideas or the ability to bring about a successful revolution. Once we begin political intervention in a country, we are letting ourselves in for trouble. So we usually take an easy, though unsatisfactory, way out.

Thus we see that the ecological view of foreign intervention is essentially conservative. The realities of foreign aid should remind us of the situation in medicine a century ago. A wise biochemist named L. J. Henderson once remarked that until 1905, a patient who chose a physician at random was worse off than he would have been had he not called in a physician. Since 1905, however, medicine has steadily been more helpful. We have heard many horror stories about poverty in the past, but not many people realize that poverty was once a blessing, medically speaking. According to an account of the way physicians treated Charles II of England in his last illness, it would have taken a superman to survive their attentions. Had King Charles been unable to afford medical attention, he would have lived longer.

I submit that foreign intervention is, at the present time, approximately in the position of medicine several centuries ago. Prior to this century, the best physicians followed a wise injunction, *primum non nocere* (first of all, do no harm). In most cases the physician was best advised to give his patient a placebo so that the patient thought he was receiving good treatment. A medicine that would have a real effect could kill him. A physician who gave nothing but placebos during his entire life could earn a great reputation. And he didn't kill as many people as his more ambitious colleagues.

Most of the time, the kindest thing we can do for other people is refrain from intervening in their lives. We are bemused by the cliché, "the global village." Just because television shows us what is happening ten thousand miles away does not mean that we can prevent its happening, not without causing worse to happen. We are too easily panicked by the expostulation, "But we can't just sit back and do nothing!" We forget not only the wisdom of *primum non nocere* but also a basic rule of ecology—namely, we can never do merely one thing.

We cannot just save people's lives. In the act of saving lives, we do something else, the substance of which depends on the country and on the particular circumstances. One important pattern, repeated many places in the world, has been made clear in the book *Losing Ground* by Erik Eckholm of the Worldwatch Institute.[1] Eckholm describes what is now going on in the tropical highlands. About 10 percent of the world's population lives in these regions, but what happens there affects 30 percent of the world's people, those in the lowlands. Highlands are now being deforested at a rapidly accelerating rate. When trees are removed from steep slopes, a series of events is set in motion which can only have a disastrous ending. Once the trees are gone the

1. Erik P. Eckholm, *Losing Ground: Environmental Stress and World Food Prospects* (New York: W. W. Norton, 1976).

soil rapidly erodes away, washing downhill. If there are ter-
raced areas below, terraces built up over thousands of years,
they may be washed away almost overnight. Only with great
effort can they ever be rebuilt. When the water reaches the
lowlands the silt clogs irrigation systems, making more work
for the lowland people. Silt fills in behind expensive dams,
and a dam designed to last one hundred years may last only
twenty-five. Ordinarily, soil on highland slopes acts like a
sponge, absorbing heavy rains and letting the water squeeze
out gradually over a period of weeks, which makes for a prolonged but not very high flood. Once the soil is gone from
the highlands, a quick flood with a high crest occurs, causing much more loss of life and property.

The floods that now take place in Bangladesh are clearly
far worse than they were three hundred years ago, though
there is no indication that the weather has changed signific-
antly. The greater severity is caused by the deforestation of
the Himalayas above Bangladesh. Floods now called normal frequently cover one-third of the land, and sometimes
they cover as much as two-thirds of the land, bringing about
immense loss of life and property, including badly needed
crops. It is useless to talk of reforesting the highlands, because they are too steep, too bare; the damage is irrevocable.

Why does this happen? Basically for one reason: there are
too many people in the highlands. People need not only
food but energy. Highland people cut down trees so that
they can cook their rice. When there are too many people
they must deforest their land, even though the patrimony of
their children is thereby destroyed. They are trapped. Well-
intentioned interveners from rich countries help close the
trap faster by saving lives with western medicine and more
productive agriculture. By increasing the population in the
highlands, western interveners have diminished the quality
of life in both highlands and lowlands. Posterity has been
harmed even more.

It is axiomatic in science that if you ask the wrong question, you will get the wrong answer. For example, the development of chemistry was held up for many many decades by asking questions couched in terms of the mistaken concept of phlogiston. Progress was made only when this concept was abandoned in favor of the oxygen combustion concept. Concerning foreign intervention, the wrong concept is world hunger. It all looks very simple; if more food is produced, then hunger disappears. Unfortunately, any extra food will soon be converted into more people who will create a larger demand for food. Thus hunger returns, only at a higher level. To be blunt, the hunger of an individual can indeed be remedied by more food, but the hunger of a population cannot. A hungry, growing population plus more food results in a larger, still-hungry population at a later date. As ecologists see it, the basic concept is not world hunger but rather carrying capacity. Looking at each area we should ask, what is the carrying capacity of this land?

There is no single figure for the carrying capacity of a land; that number is a function of the quality of life one insists on living. What we call a high-quality life requires large inputs of materials and energy. High standards reduce the carrying capacity; if we are willing to settle for lower standards, the carrying capacity is greater. Standards and capacity are inversely interrelated; they cannot be separately considered. The joint answer implies, of course, a specified technology, but to be realistic, our plans should always be made on the basis of existing technology. Today's children can't be fed on tomorrow's technology, which may be disappointing when it comes.

Foreign intervention should observe this rule: Never encourage the actual population to exceed the carrying capacity. There are two good reasons for this advice. First, if population is allowed to exceed carrying capacity, the quality of life will deteriorate. Second (and even more important), transgressing carrying capacity in the present reduces carrying capacity in the future. The reduction will very likely be irrevocable. Those who take the interests of posterity to heart should stop talking about world hunger and govern their international activities in light of the imperatives of regional carrying capacity.

Common sense dictates that we should always try to solve a problem on the most local scale possible. Of course, there are some problems for which the local scale is the entire earth, for example, the pollution of the atmosphere by carbon dioxide, fluorocarbons of aerosol bombs, or nitrogen oxides from supersonic aircraft. I need hardly remind you that when global solutions are called for, the political impediments to the application of knowledge are most serious. So let us not seek preferentially to set any problem into a global framework. Yet that is precisely what the fashionable rhetoric of the moment does. One world, the shrinking globe, world hunger, the global village, and the interdependence of peoples—all tend to turn our attention away from conceivably productive local approaches to an almost certainly nonproductive global approach, which amounts to a sort of Freudian death wish as far as practical accomplishment is concerned.

The global approach cannot work at the present time because there is no globally responsible power. Perhaps some day there will be, but the solutions to our problems cannot await the millenium. We must work with the responsible entities at hand, and of these the largest units are sovereign nations. If population can be controlled anywhere, it can be controlled only by nations—*some* nations. And it will remain globally uncontrolled if the uncontrolled growth of some nations is perpetually financed by others. The idea that a sovereign nation should be responsible was accepted without question until about 1949 when President Truman said that the United States would take on its own shoulders the problems of world hunger. Surely, however, the experience of the last twenty-five years should convince us that global solutions are too difficult and that we should return to the assumption that nations are responsible for their own survival.

Responsibility is painful, but it brings strength to those who accept it, as in the following true story.[2] Five years ago, a rugby team from Uruguay set off for Chile in an airplane. On the way, their plane crashed in the mountains. Most of the young people were still left alive with half of the hull of the plane. Up in the Andes, they were miles from any-where, and nobody knew their location. Unfortunately, they did not have an electronics expert with them, so they could not operate the radio-sending equipment; but they did manage to get a radio receiver working. The more severely wounded stayed inside the broken cabin protecting them-selves from the weather, while the healthier people were outside the plane, listening to the radio. Day after day they heard that the Chilean air force was searching for them. After many fruitless days the Chileans called off the search. The people outside the plane were thunderstruck by the an-nouncement. One of them asked whether the people inside the plane should be told. Another said no, because it would break their hearts. But one stood up and said that they must be told. He walked to the open side of the cabin and shouted inside that there was some good news that the search had been called off. From inside the cabin there were groans and the inevitable question, "Why the hell is that good news?" To this the reply was given, "Because it means that we're going to get out of here on our own." And they did. Not all of them, but many of them. You may not like the implied message, but think of the other possibility. If they had not known that they were on their own, they would have sat there until all would have died. Once they knew that they could get no help, they exerted all their ability and strength to survive.

Such is the position of any poor country. There is no

2. Piers Paul Read, *Alive* (New York: J. P. Lippincott, 1973).

country so poor that it cannot support a very considerable population, provided that population does not exceed the carrying capacity. India, a classic example, has a population three times as great as that of the United States, though their territory is only one-third as great. If, instead of 600 million people, India had only 70 million people, its population would be in clover. Apparently, for many centuries its population was only about 100 million. Their troubles started compounding about three hundred years ago, when the population rose above 100 million.

A significant comparison can be made between India and China. Reading the newspapers and magazines of fifty years ago, I think that you would come to the conclusion that India and China were then about equally miserable and that their prospects seemed equally hopeless. Then about thirty years ago, the Communists came into power, and the country suffered a revolution. Out of all the troubles came a centralized government, which under Mao Tse Tung committed itself, as early as 1947, to a policy of self-reliance. During the fifties, Russia gave foreign aid to China for a short while. There was a political falling-out, and Russians were thrown out of the country. That was the end of all foreign intervention in China. The United States did not inflict foreign aid on these people because we did not recognize the existence of mainland China. We could see the 16 million people in Taiwan, but not the 500 million just to the west of them. We said those people did not exist. So, for the past twenty-five years, China has had no help from any other country.

In contrast, for the past twenty-five years India has had "help" on a massive scale from many countries. I use the prejudicial word *help* simply because it is customary. But really, in terms of the facts of the case, was it help? Or, to look at the matter a different way, could China have survived if we had helped her the way we helped India? I think it is doubtful. China was like those Uruguayan rugby players who knew they were on their own. The country took losses, just as the rugby players did. Millions of people died, and production problems were compounded by political difficulties; but at least the problems were all internal. With the outside world inhibited from doing harm (in the name of doing good), China made it on its own.

Does the old-fashioned medical motto of *primum non nocere* entirely rule out intervention? Perhaps not. Now and then we might *cautiously* intervene in another country, if we are absolutely sure that we can do good. What we need most is a method of postauditing the results of our efforts so that we can know when we make mistakes. Such an audit needs to be made by an independent agency. [3]

The best chance for the maximum survival of the world's population with the minimal damage to the carrying capacity will result from following the policy that each country must be self-reliant. I do not say self-sufficient, because no modern country can be self-sufficient. Every country has to obtain some things from other countries. If it trades the goods it has in excess for those that it needs, then it is self-reliant. Only the goal of self-reliance makes ecological sense in the long run. I believe also that, *in the long run*, the pursuit of this goal is the most humane policy we can follow.

3. William and Elizabeth Paddock, *We Don't Know How* (Ames: Iowa State University Press, 1973).

Ethical Implications of
Limits to Global Development

HERMAN E. DALY

INTRODUCTION   This essay deals with judgments of fact and judgments of value. The judgments of fact are discussed in section 1 in terms of an "impossibility theorem" that denies the possibility of generalizing United States resource consumption standards either to all countries or to many future generations. Since there is substantial disagreement on this theorem, I call it a judgment of fact—a judgment, in the face of uncertainty and disagreement, about the way the world really is. I do not doubt that much of this disagreement on facts stems from differing basic religious commitments about the nature of man and creation, though I suspect that simple ignorance also plays a significant role. Nevertheless, the question at issue is a question of *fact*, even though our perceptions are inevitably shaped and filtered by our basic sense of ultimate value.

Depending on the judgment of fact made (acceptance or rejection of the impossibility theorem), we bring upon ourselves two very different alternative sets of problems requiring judgments of value. This is the topic of section 2. At first, it appears that if the theorem is true, the ethical issues to be faced are so difficult that the wish to escape them may foster disbelief in the theorem. Upon reflection, however, the ethical problems arising from rejection of the impossibility theorem may seem to be, in the long run, even more intractable. Our ethical traditions offer guidance only to mortal creatures, not to a species that would graduate from creaturely existence and acquire godlike powers of creation. The rejection of the impossibility theorem would allow us to evade traditional ethical problems of extreme difficulty, but only at the cost of stepping outside the ethical tradition of humanity into a void.

1. AN IMPOSSIBILITY THEOREM   The laws of thermo-dynamics, the fixed solar flux, the intricately coevolved interdependences of the ecosystem, and the pattern of geologic concentrations of minerals in the earth's crust—all combine to set a limit on the total number of people (or more exactly, "person-years") that can be lived in the high-consumption industrial life-style generally identified with development. Economic development as it is understood today cannot be applied to all nations or even to very many future generations in our own country. The starting point in our thinking about development should be an impossi-bility theorem, namely, that an American-style high-consumption standard for a world of four billion people is impossible. Even if the standard could be attained, it would be very short-lived. It is even less possible to support an ever-growing standard of consumption for an ever-growing population.[1]

Impossibility theorems are very important in science. They keep us from wasting time. If a mathematician can prove that a problem has no solution, he saves an immense amount of time by not looking for it. The most basic laws of science are statements of impossibility: It is impossible to create or destroy matter-energy, it is impossible to travel faster than the speed of light, it is impossible to have per-

1. See also Nathan Keyfitz, "Population Theory and Doctrine: A Historical Survey," in W. Peterson (ed.), *Readings in Population* (New York: Macmillan, 1972), and "World Resources and the World Middle Class," *Scientific American*, CCXXXV (July, 1976), 28–35. See especially Nicholas Georgescu-Roegen, "Inequality, Limits and Growth from a Bioeconomic Viewpoint," *Review of Social Economy*, XXXV (December 1977).

petual motion, it is impossible for an organism to live in a medium consisting entirely of its own waste products, it is impossible to measure anything without in some way interfering with the thing measured. The great success of physical science is in large part due to its intelligent refusal to attempt the impossible. Paradoxically, this very success has been taken by the public as proof that nothing is impossible!

The impossibility theorem concerning world development along the United States pattern ultimately derives from the basic impossibility statements of science, especially the second law of thermodynamics. Consider that it requires about one-third of the world's annual extraction of nonrenewable resources to support that 6 percent of the world's population in the United States at the per capita level to which it is thought the rest of the world should become accustomed. This means that if United States levels of technology could prevail worldwide, present resource flows could support at most 18 percent of the world's population at United States levels, with nothing left over for the other 82 percent. Without the labor services of the lower 82 percent the rich 18 percent would not be as rich as we might think. There is an unavoidable relative dimension in the concept of riches. As John Ruskin told us, "The force of the guinea you have in your pocket depends wholly on the default of a guinea in your neighbor's pocket."[2]

The solution, some will argue, is simply to increase world resource flows by some multiple that would allow world per capita use to equal United States per capita use. The necessary multiple turns out to be a factor of about 6 or 7.[3] Current rates of energy and materials use are already doing seri-

2. John Ruskin, *Unto This Last: Four Essays on the First Principles of Political Economy*, ed. Lloyd J. Hubenka (Lincoln: University of Nebraska Press, 1967 [1860]), 30.

3. Let M be the required factor and R be world annual resource usage. For world per capita usage to equal U.S. per capita usage requires that:

$$\frac{M \cdot R}{4 \times 10^9} = \frac{1/3\ R}{2.1 \times 10^8} \rightarrow M = 6.35$$

ous damage to the life-support capacity of the globe. What would be the ecological result of a sixfold increase? The six-fold increase in resource flows requires an extension of the United States level of capital stocks for processing and trans-forming that enlarged resource flow. This capital stock must be accumulated out of a previous larger flow. To supply the rest of the world with the average per capita "standing crop" of industrial metals already embodied in existing artifacts in the ten richest nations would require more than sixty years' production of these metals at 1970 rates.[4] But even granting the miracle of instantaneous capital accumulation out of nothing, the problem is still understated because a sixfold increase in flows of net energy and usable minerals will re-quire much more than a sixfold increase in gross energy use and gross materials extraction, thanks to diminishing re-turns. Since environmental impact is a function of the gross flows, not the net flows, we can be sure that the impact would increase by much more than a factor of 6. It is sober-ing to reflect that as we shift from mining ore of, say, 1 per-cent concentration to one-half of 1 percent, the gross mate-rial flow per net output of the mineral will double. The energy requirement per unit will usually more than double. If the goal of applying current United States resource con-sumption levels to all countries is not feasible, then how much more unrealistic is it to expect that an ever-growing United States level can be applied to all nations and all fu-ture generations!

The ecosphere in its physical dimensions approximates a steady-state open system. Its stock of materials is constant and its rate of throughput of solar energy is constant. The human economy is a growing subsystem of this larger steady-state system. As the economy grows, an increasingly large percentage of the ecosphere is converted into econo-

4. Harrison Brown, "Human Materials Production as a Process in the Bios-phere," *Scientific American*, CCXXIII (September, 1970), 195–208.

sphere, and we take over the conscious management of more energy and material flows that were previously under the automatic management of nature. This process is clearly limited by the finitude of the total ecosphere, but it is much more stringently limited by the growing complexity of the managerial role we are assuming and the costly social discipline and sacrifice of personal freedom imposed by that explosive complexity. Observe the problems of nuclear safeguards.

At least some economists are beginning to express doubts about the traditional goal of economic development. Richard Wilkinson writes, "Predictions of when the resources which modern industrial technology depends on will run out are usually within the same time scale as the predictions of when many underdeveloped countries may reach maturity."[5] But such nascent doubts are exceptional. Orthodox economists have not yet understood the problem. For example, former presidential economic advisor Paul W. McCracken says: "The action most urgently needed in the world economy is for the stronger economies to be willing to accept higher levels of living. Their reluctance to do so seems to be of Calvinistic proportions."[6]

In other words, if the rich would only consume more, they would buy more of everything, including the products of the poor, and the poor would be better off. The only problem, evidently, is insufficient aggregate demand. Keynesian pump-priming is the paradigm within which world development is viewed. Absolute limits to resource supplies and the concept of distributive justice are totally neglected. It apparently does not matter if the rich get richer faster than the poor get richer, as long as the absolute con-

5. Richard Wilkinson, *Poverty and Progress: An Ecological Perspective on Economic Development* (New York: Praeger, 1973), 216.
6. Paul W. McCracken, "A Way Out of the World's Slump," *Wall Street Journal*, September 17, 1975, 24.

sumption of all is growing. McCracken and many other economists for whom he is the distinguished spokesman are obviously unconcerned about any impossibility theorem. They do not even entertain the thought that the rich might consume less and thus free resources for the poor, who could create their own markets by selling necessities to each other, instead of having to sell ever more extravagant luxuries to those rich but abstemious "Calvinists."

McCracken's views are not ad hoc or idiosyncratic, but rather they follow logically from the standard economic thinking of our day. Consider the following statement from *Scarcity and Growth,* the most influential book on resource economics in the last twenty years:

Science, by making the resource base more homogeneous, erases the restrictions once thought to reside in the lack of homogeneity. In a neo-Ricardian world, it seems, the particular resources with which one starts increasingly become a matter of indifference. . . . Advances in fundamental science have made it possible to take advantage of the uniformity of matter-energy—a uniformity that makes it feasible without preassignable limit to escape the quantitative constraints imposed by the character of the earth's crust. The reservation of particular resources for later use, therefore, may contribute little to the welfare of future generations. [7]

It is not the uniformity of matter-energy that makes for usefulness, however, but precisely the opposite. Nonuniformity, differences in concentrations and in temperatures, makes for usefulness. If all materials and energy were uniformly distributed in thermodynamic equilibrium, the resulting homogeneous resource base would be no resource at all. There would be a complete absence of potential for any process, including life. The mere fact that matter and energy may be reducible to a fundamental homogeneous building block, even if it were true, is of little significance if the potential for arranging those blocks is

7. Harold Barnett and Chandler Morse, *Scarcity and Growth: The Economics of Natural Resource Availability* (Baltimore: Johns Hopkins Press for Resources for the Future, 1963), 11.

scarce, as the entropy law tells us is the case.[8] Only Maxwell's Sorting Demon could turn a pile of atoms, quarks, or
whatever, into a resource. And the entropy law tells us that
Maxwell's demon does not exist. The economists' notion of
infinite substitutability of abundant for scarce resources
seems to bear some resemblance to the alchemists' dream of
converting base metals into gold. All you have to do is rear-
range atoms! That the fundamental physical root of scarcity
lies in the very potential for rearrangement is somehow
overlooked.

Another example of the mind-set that fails to consider the
impossibility theorem comes in the first sentence of a major
review of the literature of environmental economics. The
authors state that "man has probably always worried about
his environment because he *was once* totally dependent on
it" (emphasis supplied).[9] "Was once totally dependent"
seems to imply that we are no longer totally dependent. To
be less dependent on the environment would require a reduction in the volume of our imports from and exports to
the environment. That volume has been increasing, not decreasing. Furthermore, the environment's composition has
shifted away from renewables and on to nonrenewables.
Our dependence on the environment, therefore, has not
only increased but has also become more precarious.
Pushed to its extreme, the idea of independence from the
environment conflicts with the second law of thermodynamics, because it means cutting off all exchanges, or
reducing the matter-energy throughput to zero. Frederick
Soddy, Nobel laureate in chemistry and a heretical economist, put it very well: "Life derives the whole of its physical energy or power, not from anything self-contained in
living matter, and still less from an external deity, but solely

8. Nicholas Georgescu-Roegen, *The Entropy Law and the Economic Process* (Cambridge, Mass.: Harvard University Press, 1971).
9. Anthony Fisher and Frederick Peterson, "The Environment in Economics: A Survey" *Journal of Economic Literature*, XIV (March, 1976), 1.

from the inanimate world. It is dependent for all the necessities of its physical continuance upon the principles of the steam engine. The principles and ethics of human convention must not run counter to those of thermodynamics."[10]

Lack of respect for the principles of the steam engine is rampant in economics, as we have seen. Another example comes from Harvard economist Richard Zeckhauser, who, in an article defending economic growth, noted parenthetically that "recycling is not the solution for oil, because the alternate technology of nuclear power generation is cheaper."[11] The reason energy is never recycled has nothing to do with relative prices but everything to do with the entropy law. The implicit idea that energy will be recycled whenever relative prices are "right" is no doubt extreme, but is indicative of the standard myth that if only prices are right everything else will be right. It is easy to be a technological optimist if one is innocent of physical first principles.

Soddy summed up the confusions of economists on this score some fifty years ago: "Debts are subject to the laws of mathematics rather than physics. Unlike wealth, which is subject to the laws of thermodynamics, debts do not rot with old age and are not consumed in the process of living. On the contrary, they grow at so much per cent per annum by the well-known laws of simple and compound interest. . . . As a result of this confusion between wealth and debt we are invited to contemplate a millenium where people live off the interest of their mutual indebtedness."[12] We suffer from money fetishism. We identify the measure of wealth with wealth itself, which is like identifying a clock with time. The more clocks, the more time; the more monetary debt, the more wealth!

10. Frederick Soddy, *Cartesian Economics: The Bearing of Physical Science Upon State Stewardship* (London: Hendersons, 1922), 9.
11. Richard Zeckhauser, "The Risks of Growth," *Daedalus*, CII (Fall, 1973), 117.
12. Frederick Soddy, *Wealth, Virtual Wealth and Debt* (London: George Allen and Unwin, 1926), 68, 89.

Recently D. R. Helliwell felt it necessary to remind us that money does not actually "work." Only people, other animals, plants, the sun, the moon, and the earth do any effective work. Money represents, very loosely, society's assessment of the value of the work done by any individual. There is no reason to expect the amount of money in real terms to increase merely by lending it to a bank or to anyone else for twenty years, unless it is able to tap the work done by nonhuman agencies without increasing the costs of other users (either now or in the future), or unless it is used to develop more efficient methods of producing goods. Calculations of compound interest, by abstracting from the above qualifications, quickly lead to a state in which everyone "could stop investing, stop working, and each draw an annual income of £11,650 in perpetuity."[13] This, Helliwell submits, "is sheer nonsense."

Many growth economists would probably try to escape this difficulty by appealing to technology, that is, by using the money "to develop more efficient methods of producing goods." But many of the technological triumphs of the recent past fail the first test, of not "increasing costs of other users either now or in the future." True increases in efficiency are possible (but not unlimited), and they are not to be found along the path of ever-growing resource usage. Recent technical progress represents "improvements in the pump, rather than the well," to borrow a phrase from Aldo Leopold.[14]

The faith of the Middle Ages in Divine Providence was weak compared to the faith the modern world has in "provident technology." The "second coming" of Prometheus, many believe, will redeem us from the fallen state of subjection to the impossibility theorem. Prometheus will be incarnate in the Green Revolution, in nuclear power, in

13. D. R. Helliwell, "The End of the Bank-rate?" *Environmental Conservation*, IV (Summer, 1977), 130, 131.
14. *Ibid.*, 130.

space exploration, and finally in the greatest of all technical fixes, genetic engineering. Witness the ecstatic vision of the famous social scientist Kingsley Davis: "Deliberate [genetic] control, once begun would soon benefit science and technology, which in turn would facilitate further hereditary improvement, which again would extend science, and so on in a self-reinforcing spiral without limit. In other words, when man has conquered his own biological evolution he will have laid the basis for conquering everything else. The universe will be his, at last." [15]

One wonders precisely *who* will be master of the universe, for when man has conquered his own biological evolution, victor and vanquished are the same. What is most likely is that some men will have conquered the biological evolution of other men, and in so doing will themselves be in danger of having stepped into an ethical void. [16] This is the case if one believes, as many do, that biological evolution determines moral values. If moral values are to be the artifacts of those who control evolution, then they cannot simultaneously serve as independent principles for guiding the choices of the controllers. To the extent that the controllers seek to promote some traditional moral values, they are the servants of past evolution and are not independent controllers of the process. But once they become 100 percent controller and 0 percent servant, they will have no purpose other than whim, and they will have entered an ethical void. What is striking about Davis' statement is the total devotion to Prometheus for the benefit of science and technology, even to the extent of being willing to reprogram our very genetic inheritance to serve, not God or mankind, but Prometheus. Whoever said we live in an irreligious age? It is idolatrous perhaps, but the intense de-

15. Kingsley Davis, "Sociological Aspects of Genetic Control," in W. Peterson (ed.), *Readings in Population* (New York: Macmillan, 1972), 379.

16. See C. S. Lewis, *The Abolition of Man* (New York: Macmillan, 1957).

votion of the scientistic pagans to what Malcolm Muggeridge has called the Church of Christ Economist certainly puts orthodox Christians to shame.

In addition to this religiously based denial by the cult of Prometheus, class conflicts also make it politically convenient to deny the impossibility theorem. In rich countries, continued growth in per capita consumption is what buys off social conflict. Growth is a substitute for redistribution, or an attempt to substitute technics for ethics. Facing up to redistribution is too painful; it is easier to lay burnt offerings of our intelligence at the feet of Prometheus and pray for redemption from the original sin of entropic degradation. Instead of "Let my people go," the modern Moses cries, "Let my people grow!" and adds, "so that they may never have to learn about sharing and moderation."

This religious imagery may seem fanciful, but fundamentally it is proper. The same devotion to Prometheus is found in the Soviet Union. The Marxist tenet that the New Socialist Man can emerge only on the material basis of overwhelming abundance makes anathema of any impossibility theorem concerning growth. Solzhenitsyn's arguments urging the rejection of infinite progress dogma, in his *Letter to the Soviet Leaders*, evidently fell on ears deaf to such cardinal heresy. [17]

It is understandable that underdeveloped countries are not yet willing to give up their plans for growth in per capita resource consumption, but it is less acceptable that some Third World elites should be so half-hearted about limiting population growth. The ruling class limits its own progeny, but is often unenthusiastic about limiting the population of its laboring-class majorities, which provide a subsidy for industrial growth, as well as cheap farm labor and an abundant source of domestic servants. Foxes seldom advocate

17. Aleksandr Solzhenitsyn, *Letter to the Soviet Leaders* (New York: Harper and Row, 1974), Chap. 3.

birth control for rabbits. The mythology of technical om-
nipotence is by itself very strong, but when backed up by
class interests in avoiding the radical policies required by an
equitable steady state, it becomes a full-fledged idolatry.

2. ETHICAL IMPLICATIONS OF THE IMPOSSIBILITY THEOREM

If the number of person-years of industrially developed,
high consumption living is in fact limited, then we cannot
avoid questions about how this limited total of person-years
should be apportioned: among nations?, among social
classes?, among races?, among generations?, among individuals?

For the growth paradigm the answers are easy, too easy.
There is no problem of apportioning among nations. The
best thing the rich can do for the poor is to consume more
not less (recall McCracken's statement). The same idea
applies also to apportioning between social classes. And the
best thing one generation can do for the next is to bequeath
it a larger capital stock accumulated by rapid growth. No
need to worry about depleted resources if, as Harold Barnett
and Chandler Morse claimed, science has removed the
"constraints imposed by the character of the earth's crust."
Growth is so convenient—more for all with sacrifice by
none, vouchsafed by the amazing grace of compound
interest!

But further questions arise if we accept the impossibility
theorem. To what extent should subhuman life be sacrificed in exchange for more person-years of developed living? Not all subhuman life is supportive of man; some of it
is competitive. Currently we fail to respect even the subhuman life on which we depend. If we can learn to appreciate
the instrumental value of subhuman life for human beings,
perhaps we can then go on to consider its intrinsic value. If
a man is worth many sparrows, (Matt. 10:31), it must be
taken for granted that the sparrow's value is not zero. Are
we justified in examining sparrows if that adds a few

person-years of developed living? How many sparrow-years
of life are worth one person-year? How many sparrow-years
are worth the difference between one person-year of luxurious living and one person-year of frugal living?

What are the trade-offs between present and future
person-years? Could not the total number of person-years
lived, at any given consumption level from now until extinction, be maximized by spreading people out over many
generations so as to avoid the destruction of long-run carrying capacity that results from having too many people alive
at the same time?

What is the price of additional simultaneous lives now in
terms of future sequential lives sacrificed? Advocates of zero
or negative population growth are often labeled misan-
thropic or antihuman. But they could logically argue that
they are seeking to maximize the number of human lives
lived over the long run at some acceptable standard. There
is nothing wrong with twenty billion, or a hundred billion
people, as long as they are not all alive at once. Too many
alive at once means a reduction in total person-years lived
over time, as well as a reduction in present standards. It is
the population boosters and economic growth maximizers
who are antilife.

What is the price of present luxury in terms of future lives
sacrificed? Georgescu-Roegen forces us to recognize that
"every time we produce a Cadillac we do it at the cost of
decreasing the number of human lives in the future."[18] By
producing plows instead of Cadillacs we enable more people
to live off solar energy for a longer period of time. Terrestrial
minerals, if used for tapping permanent solar energy rather
than for direct consumption, increase the number of
person-years ever to be lived. But the same is true for a Volks-
wagen or a bicycle, though the number of future lives sac-

18. Nicholas Georgescu-Roegen, "The Entropy Law and the Economic
Problem," in H. E. Daly (ed.), *Toward a Steady-State Economy* (San Francisco:
W. H. Freeman, 1973), 46.

rificed is presumably less. Indeed, even present lives compete with present Cadillacs for present resources. Oil can be fed to agricultural machinery or to automobiles, and land can be used to produce food for homo sapiens or to produce grain alcohol for *mechanistra automobilica.*

Should we worry about the future at all until the basic needs of all presently existing people have been met? Can we assume the responsibility of meeting the basic needs of present people without accepting the responsibility for limiting procreation? How can the limited right to procreate be distributed in a community that controls its population? If, however, we believe that the human race is very likely to destroy the world in the next fifty years, then it would be both uneconomic and immoral to make any sacrifices for a nonexistent beneficiary. The rule then would be to consume and procreate to the maximum while the world lasts. Too much pessimism, as well as too much optimism, leads to extravagance.

Even more perplexing is the problem of how the limited total of person-years should be allocated among persons. Is it better to have ten people living sixty years each, or six people living a hundred years each? Should our limited medical resources be devoted to increasing average life expectancy at age forty or age eighty?

Probably the main value of questions such as these lies *not* in the prospects for an answer, but in the intellectual humility they inspire. We should not expect rigorous environmental cost-benefit studies from economists like me who have no idea how many sparrows are worth a person, or how many future person-years are worth a Cadillac. One even hesitates to raise such questions for fear that some econometrician will rush out and construct a model for maximizing the discounted value of a weighted sum of years lived by all species from now on. We are better off relying on moral insight, traditional wisdom, and prayerful meditation than on the arcane numerology of one-eyed Pythagoreans.

To indicate a more reasonable approach let me suggest the following principle: Sufficient wealth, efficiently maintained and allocated and equitably distributed, not maximum production growth, is the proper economic aim. The concept of a steady-state economy and its institutions for achieving stability, efficiency, and equity have been discussed elsewhere.[19] The issue for now is the meaning of *sufficiency*. How much is enough? It makes no sense to speak of sufficiency except in relation to some purpose. Sufficient for what? Sufficient for living a good life. Regarding the meaning of a good life, the concept of sufficiency leads us to the basic religious and philosophical question: What is the nature of the good, and how can mankind attain it? We have ceased to ask this question seriously. We are guided only by a vague feeling that more is better than less, and we cannot get enough mainly because we do not know what we are looking for or why we want it. As long as it seemed possible that there would be more forever, we could escape the basic question or else answer it simplistically by saying that good is more for all forever. But the impossibility theorem closes that escape route.

The old Benthamite rule, the greatest good for the greatest number, is not a bad principle. But in striving to make it operational, economists have reduced unmeasurable good to measurable goods and services, or per capita product. Even in this reduced form, two problems exist. First, as is well known, the dictum contains one *greatest* too many. We cannot maximize for two variables at the same time. Numbers and per capita product can be traded off against each other. For one of the *greatests* we must substitute *sufficient*. Second, it makes a big difference whether

19. H. E. Daly, *Steady-State Economics: The Economics of Biophysical Equilibrium and Moral Growth* (San Francisco: W. H. Freeman, 1977).

number refers to the number of people simultaneously alive or to the cumulative number ever to live. To conform with the argument of this paper, the principle must be revised to read *sufficient per capita product for the greatest number over time.* Unfortunately, the rule of right action in the growth economy seems to be the greatest per capita product for the greatest number now, which is both logically and ethically flawed.

I cannot pretend to be saddened by the impossibility theorem. It forces us to ask the big questions, and it is only in living with these questions and seriously pondering them that we can hope for true moral progress. As Soddy said, "The principles and ethics of human convention must not run counter to those of thermodynamics." For too long our implicit economic ethics have run counter to thermodynamics, and we now face a large but welcome job of reconstruction. As we come to understand more fully the true cost of more person-years of present luxurious living in the United States, we may lower our estimates of what constitutes a sufficient population and a sufficient per capita material base for a good life. Insisting on the necessity of bringing the concept of sufficiency into economic theory may sound utopian, but it would hardly be more utopian than the current belief that economics has no need for the concept. As J. K. Galbraith remarked, "It is silly for grown men to concern themselves mightily with satisfying an appetite and close their eyes to the obvious and obtrusive question of whether the appetite is excessive."[20]

To deal with this obvious and obtrusive question requires some reference to the concept of sufficiency, by which we define *excessive.* Because economists do not want to deal with that question, they pretend that it is either meaningless or definable only by each individual for himself. Clearly,

20. J. K. Galbraith, "How Much Should a Country Consume?" in Henry Jarrett (ed.), *Perspectives on Conservation* (Baltimore: Johns Hopkins Press, 1958), 98.

sufficiency is not definable in strictly objective terms. Its definition requires a moral consensus concerning what is meant by a good life.

But where is this moral consensus to come from? Ultimately, it must come from a dogmatic belief in objective value. If values are subjective or thought merely to be cultural artifacts, then there is nothing objective to which appeal can be made or around which a consensus might be formed. Consensus based upon what everyone recognizes to be a convenient cultural myth (such as belief in Santa Claus) would not bear much stress. Only real, objective values can command consensus in a sophisticated, self-analytical society. We have no guarantee that objective value can be clarified or that, once clarified, it would be accorded the consensus that it merits. But without faith in the existence of an objective hierarchy of value and in our ability at least vaguely to perceive it, we must resign ourselves to being driven by the force of technological determinism into an unchosen and perhaps unbearable future. On what other grounds is technical determinism to be resisted?

In C. S. Lewis' words, "A dogmatic belief in objective value is necessary to the very idea of a rule which is not tyranny or an obedience which is not slavery."[21] The same insight underlies Edmund Burke's famous dictum that "society cannot exist unless a controlling power upon will and appetite be placed somewhere, and the less of it there is within, the more there must be without."[22] Control from within can only result from obedience to objective value. If interior restraints on will and appetite diminish, then exterior restraints, coercive police powers, and Malthusian positive checks must increase. In Burke's words, "Men of

21. Lewis, *The Abolition of Man*, 46.
22. Edmund Burke, "Letter to a Member of the National Assembly," in *The Works of the Right Honorable Edmund Burke* (12 vols.; Boston: Little, Brown, 1865), IV, 51–52.

intemperate minds cannot be free. Their passions forge their fetters."[23]

The greatest of all reasons for pessimism about the course of human affairs is that the very notion of *dogmatic* belief in *objective* value automatically shuts the minds of most modern intellectuals. Why is this so? Probably because *dogmatic* has come to be almost synonymous with *egotistic*, and because the term *objective value* has connotations of absolutism and intolerance. The confusions underlying these two misinterpretations have been well stated by others. G. K. Chesterton informs us:

> To be dogmatic and to be egotistic are not only not the same thing, they are opposite things. Suppose, for instance that a vague skeptic eventually joins the Catholic church. In that act he has at the same moment become less egotistic and more dogmatic. The dogmatist is by the nature of the case not egotistical, because he believes that there is some solid, obvious and objective truth outside him which he has perceived and which he invites all men to perceive. And the egotist is in the majority of cases not dogmatic, because he has no need to isolate one of his notions as being related to the truth; all his notions are equally interesting because they are related to him. The true egotist is as much interested in his own errors as in his own truth; the dogmatist is interested only in the truth, and only in the truth because it is true. At the most the dogmatist believes that he is in the truth; but the egotist believes that the truth, if there is such a thing, is in him.[24]

A related clarification was made by E. F. Schumacher:

> The result of the lopsided development of the last three hundred years is that Western man has become rich in means and poor in ends. The hierarchy of his knowledge has been decapitated: his will is paralyzed because he has lost any grounds on which to base a hierarchy of values. What are his highest values?
>
> A man's highest values are reached when he claims that something is good in itself, requiring no justification in terms of any higher good. Modern society prides itself on its pluralism, which means that a large number of things are admissible as "good in

23. *Ibid.*
24. G. K. Chesterton, Introduction, *Poems by John Ruskin* (London: George Routledge and Sons, n.d.), x–xi.

themselves," as ends rather than as means to an end. They are all of equal rank, all to be accorded *first priority*. If something that requires no justification may be called an "absolute," the modern world, which *claims* that everything is relative, does, in fact, worship a very large number of "absolutes.". . . Not only power and wealth are treated as goods in themselves—provided they are mine and not someone else's—but also knowledge for its own sake, speed of movement, size of market, rapidity of change, quantity of education, number of hospitals, etc., etc. In truth, none of these sacred cows is a genuine end; they are all means parading as ends. [25]

Science and technology with their rational-empirical mode of thinking have led many into a kind of scientism which seeks to debunk all knowledge that does not have a rational-empirical basis. Knowledge about ends, about objective value and right purpose derives from an "illicit" source and is believed to be "forbidden knowledge" by the priests of the scientistic inquisition. Unless this error is recognized and unless we come around to a dogmatic belief in objective value, or what Boris Pasternak called "the irresistible power of unarmed truth," then it makes no sense to concern ourselves with economics. Why strain out gnats of marginal inefficiency in the allocation of means to serve ends, while swallowing camels of total incoherence in the ordering of those ends? Indeed, if our ends are perversely ordered, then it is better for us to be inefficient in allocating means to their service.

The ethical implications of limits to global development are, if not overwhelming, at least very challenging. They are so challenging, in fact, that space colonization has been offered by respectable scientists as the inevitable way to avoid the transition to a steady, no-growth situation on earth—a situation held to be socially impossible. [26] The at-

25. E. F. Schumacher, *A Guide for the Perplexed* (New York: Harper and Row, 1977), 58.
26. See report of American Association for the Advancement of Science meeting by Walter Sullivan, "Establishment of Space Colonies Inevitable, Scientists Told," *New York Times*, February 16, 1978, 44.

tempt to evade moral problems by further growth and technological razzle-dazzle knows no limits. It is as if the human species, having lost its faith in personal immortality, now places faith in the immortality of the species. Since the species cannot pretend to immortality while it is part of a mortal earth, it must believe in flight to other galaxies. In exploring space, man really could be searching for time. How different from the traditional Christian view, which takes it for granted that the species is mortal and that the world will end, but has faith that the individual soul or spirit is in some sense immortal. Believers in personal immortality can at least claim to have had some direct spiritual experience of their own immortal nature. No one has any direct experience of the abrogation of the entropy law in some remote corner of space-time, nor do they have any consequent intimations of species immortality. It is ironic that the scientistic faith in species immortality thoroughly contradicts the most basic of all scientific laws, the entropy law, against which the idolized savior of technology is unavailing.

In conclusion, it appears to me that the impossibility theorem is true, that man must seek the eternal, not in exterior physical space, but in interior spiritual space, and that our ethical tradition must be developed on those terms. Although the fatuous dream of eternal life for the species should be rejected, a strong brotherly concern for the distant future and for not diminishing the finite number of person-years of possible life should become a primary ethical norm. Indeed, it is precisely because the total number of person-years is not infinite that we must count any diminution of total person-years as a cost to be avoided.

If, on the contrary, we reject the impossibility theorem and continue to believe in species immortality (i.e., in an infinite number of person-years of developed living), then there would be no necessary sacrifice of future life resulting from present luxury, overpopulation, or technological abuse of the environment. We in the present would have escaped the ethical problems of finite creaturely existence, but only by presuming godlike power of creation with respect to time and the physical universe. God has no need of ethics, and if the human species becomes godlike it too need not be troubled by the nagging of a vestigial conscience that evolved under conditions that will have been superseded. The ethical void entailed by rejection of the impossibility theorem will have been realized. The void is there waiting; but it takes some effort to see it, perhaps because it is so extremely and desolately empty.

Some Thoughts on the Global Food and Population Problem

ROBERT F. CHANDLER, JR.

THE POPULATION of the world has now exceeded 4 billion, and the annual growth rate continues at about 2 percent. Unfortunately, the bulk of the increase is in the poorer, less-developed nations. Unless there is either a decided reduction in the birth rate or the unfortunate event of an increased death rate, the race between food production and population will be lost.

Today (1977), in spite of the fact that the world has had three rather good crop years in a row, about 500 million people are suffering from undernutrition. Over a billion more, who are suffering from less-serious degrees of malnutrition, would indeed benefit from an improved diet. The greatest cause of hunger and malnutrition is poverty. Poor people everywhere, whether in the United States or abroad, are generally undernourished. However, by far the greatest number of underfed people are concentrated in the less-developed nations, mostly in the tropics and subtropics.

If one has not been to such countries as India and Bangladesh, he finds it difficult to visualize the great gap between those who live as we do in the United States and those who exist with incomes varying mostly between fifty and two hundred dollars a year. With the possible exception of a few cases in the Punjab, I have yet to see an overweight man or woman in rural India. I refer to the farmers themselves, not to the merchant or moneylender who may reside in a rural village.

The food and population problem might be more vividly pictured from a comparison of ourselves with Mexico, our neighbor to the south. The total land area of Mexico is about 760,000 square miles. An equivalent land area in the United States would be all of Texas and Oklahoma and the other nine states to the east and south. Comparing the populations of these eleven states and of Mexico in 1930 with the population statistics for the two areas in 1976 shows that in 1930 the population of the eleven states was 28 million, and that of Mexico was only 16 million. In 1976 the population of the eleven states was 50 million, and that of Mexico had reached 62 million. In other words, during the forty-six-year period, Mexico's population increased by 46 million, while that in an area of similar size in the United States increased by only 22 million. The gap, of course, will widen even more during the decades ahead, for Mexico's population growth rate will probably remain around 3 percent for the near future at least, while that of the United States undoubtedly will become zero in the next fifteen years or so. I make these predictions because Mexico has shown few signs of mounting a massive family planning program, and the statistics for the United States show that the current number of births per female is about 1.8, a rate insufficient to maintain the population at a constant level.

If we divide the world into two categories, developed nations and less-developed nations, we find that during the past twenty years the developed nations have shown an increased per capita food production, while the less-developed nations have produced only enough food barely to keep pace with population growth. Rice feeds about half the world's population. It is, therefore, appropriate to use rice production as an indicator of the food problem. This is especially true in Asia, where 90 percent of the world's rice is produced and consumed.

Bangladesh has an area of about 55,000 square miles, equal to the land area of Georgia. In 1960 Bangladesh had a population of 50,300,000, and Georgia had 3,943,000 inhabitants. By 1970 the population in Bangladesh had increased by 11,500,000, to reach a total of 61,800,000, while that of Georgia had increased by only 647,000, to reach a total population of only 4,590,000. The per capita production and consumption of rice in Bangladesh is about 190 kilograms of milled rice annually. There has been no increase in the per capita production of the crop since 1960. In fact, there has been a small decrease during this period. Many of us feel that countries such as Bangladesh that have very limited resources for export have only two avenues left for their economic improvement. One is to reduce their population growth rate to zero and the other (which is obviously a stopgap measure) is to increase their yields per unit area of land. Regarding the latter, the yield of rough rice in Bangladesh today is about 1.8 metric tons per hectare, while the average in Asia, including the People's Republic of China, is 2.4 metric tons per hectare. If Bangladesh *could* raise its yield level to that of the rest of Asia, it could take care of its food needs through the year 2000. But unless population growth is markedly slowed down, the increased crop yields will provide only temporary relief.

In pointing out the temporary benefits of increasing crop yields, I do not wish to create the impression that it is unimportant. Actually, it is usually quicker and easier for a nation to increase its crop yields than to decrease population growth rates. Furthermore, it is the only immediate solution to the nutrition problem in countries that have a food deficit and cannot afford to import cereal grains.

There are nations having average rice yields per hectare that are twice those of Asia as a whole. Examples are Japan, Korea, Spain, Portugal, Egypt, Australia and the United States. Regarding rice production, these nations have several things in common. They use high amounts of fertilizer, and essentially 100 percent of the rice land is irrigated. Their governments have a policy guaranteeing a minimum support price for rice; farmers know before they plant that they can make a profit if yields are good. We may compare the two extremes, Japan and Bangladesh. Japan has controlled irrigation on 98 percent of its rice land; Bangladesh has controlled water supplies on only 16 percent. Japan uses 407 kilograms of nutrients (nitrogen, phosphorus, potassium) on each hectare of arable land; the corresponding figure for Bangladesh is 20. Japan supports the price of rice at around 2.5 times the world price, but Bangladesh, I understand, does not have any guaranteed rice price.

Many economists have predicted the outcome of the world food problem through this century. Few have dared go beyond the year 2,000. Their forecasts vary with the individual; the pessimists give a gloomy outcome, and the optimists are at the other extreme. Personally, I have taken a middle course. In my opinion, the less-developed nations will continue to keep about even with their food needs, and per capita food production will remain about as it is today throughout the present century. There may well be years of scarcity when the weather is unfavorable and nations such as the United States will have to come to the rescue. I do not believe, however, that widespread, continuous, and devastating food shortages will occur during this century. As mentioned earlier, the average rice yield in Asia today is about 2.4 metric tons per hectare. If sufficient effort is made, this yield can be increased to 3.2 t/ha between 1990 and 2000. This isn't enough to provide adequate nutrition, but it will furnish enough to feed people at about the same as today's level.

Even this rather modest increase that I believe is possible will not occur unless governments are willing to invest large amounts of money in irrigation projects to permit year-round cropping in the tropics and unless fertilizer is made more readily and economically available and is used to a much larger extent than it is today. Of course, agricultural development is a complex operation, and many other factors besides irrigation and fertilizers interact to shape prospects for agricultural development. Among those factors are rural credit, farm-to-market roads, on-farm trials and demonstrations, an effective and well-supported extension organization, and off-farm employment opportunities

One of the principal reasons for having confidence that the developing world can continue to feed itself at present levels of nutrition for the remainder of this century is that during the past fifteen years new varieties of rice and wheat have been developed which, when properly managed and fertilized, have twice the yield potential of the traditional varieties. The spread of these varieties, especially in Asia, has been called the Green Revolution. It has opened new vistas for the increased production of the two most important food crops: wheat and rice. This new yield potential cannot be realized, however, without large investments in irrigation systems and fertilizer plants; the yield of these modern varieties is not much higher than that of the traditional ones if water and plant nutrient supplies are not adequate.

Obviously, if food production is to keep pace with population growth, additional energy sources and funds must be made available. It should be remembered, however, that because the less-developed nations of the world will continue to have a labor surplus for many years to come, a good share of the farming operations that are fully mechanized in America or Europe, for example, will be performed by hand. Thus the source of energy in the less-affluent nations will be the food that they grow.

The production of nitrogen fertilizer requires fossil fuel. All of mankind, whether rich or poor, must find a substitute for the dwindling supplies of petroleum, natural gas, and coal. Furthermore, farmers in poorer nations can substitute local sources of organic matter for chemical fertilizer, as is done in China. The construction of large irrigation systems and chemical fertilizer plants requires financing. Usually such projects are funded by forms of international aid. There are abundant sources of funds that can be borrowed at low interest rates from such organizations as the World Bank, the Asian Development Bank, and a number of national foreign assistance agencies in such countries as the United States, Canada, Sweden, the United Kingdom, and West Germany. The other ingredients required to transform agriculture from the traditional to the modern—credit, farm-to-market roads, adaptive research, a well-run extension service, and off-farm employment opportunities— must, however, be provided by local or national governments.

What are the predictions beyond the year 2000? Various people and organizations have made estimates of when the world's population will become constant and what the population will be at that time. The estimates that I have seen suggest that the number of people in the world will become constant somewhere around the end of the twenty-first century, or at least by the middle of the twenty-second century, and that the population at that time will be between 15 billion and 20 billion, probably nearer 15 billion.

This, of course, means that eventually we shall have to feed four times as many people as now exist on this earth. They will have to be not only fed but accommodated socially, politically, and economically. The challenge before humanity is to find ways of reaching a constant population at an earlier stage than the predictions cited above. In my opinion, the world must reach a steady state, in which population is constant and the inputs and outputs of industry and agriculture more or less equal each other.

If humanity does not reach such goals through widespread education and intelligent planning, they will be achieved in most inhumane and disastrous ways—famine, disease, rioting, and massive killing. The outlook is not bright, but there is still time to avert disaster, if people will act. Informed action is the essential need.

Distributive Justice and American Health Care

HARMON L. SMITH

THE ISSUE—in some sense, the problem—to which this essay is addressed was succinctly stated several years ago by Edgar Friedenberg: "American society is not designed to respond to needs, which is what losers have. Instead, it responds to demands, which are what winners are in a position to make."[1] The subject here is the losers, people who are not only economically deprived and disadvantaged but, largely for that reason, deprived and disadvantaged in other aspects of their existence, preeminently in medical care. I believe that this is an urgent matter of business in this society, if only because it is an item of such long and neglected standing on the national agenda.

To put the problem of being poor into perspective, I want also to observe at the outset, without diminishing my sensibility for what is at stake, that impecuniousness is only one, albeit the most obvious, of the many faces of poverty. The lack of money in this entrepreneurial, acquisitive society is typically one's ticket to poor education, poor opportunity, poor performance, and poor incentive as well as to inferior nutrition, hygiene, and health. The presumption that economics lies at the root of this problem is probably correct, as far as it goes; but if we do not recognize that the context of

1. Edgar Friedenberg, "Bad Blood," in Richard W. Wertz (ed.), *Readings on Ethical and Social Issues in Biomedicine* (Englewood Cliffs, N.J.: Prentice-Hall, 1973), 260–68.

the problem is fundamentally a human context and that economic solutions are merely means to certain ends that people themselves devise and sanction, we do not go far enough. If we simply suppose that money or goods or services, or all of these together, will provide an adequate solution, we will fail to comprehend the many subtle and insidious faces of poverty, the range of injustice and oppression encompassed by that word, and indeed the reason that poverty is a problem at all.

Being poor, that is, being needy, weak, insufficient, or lacking, is a universal human condition, and each of us, if we compare another's gifts, possessions, or capabilities with our own, is poor. What makes economic destitution simultaneously so basic and pervasive is that, in this society at least, it is increasingly the case that possession of money is precursory to virtually everything else the society has to offer. To be sure, we continue to celebrate the Horatio Alger story as an indispensable element of the American dream, and on occasion somebody seems to have had the serendipitous coincidence of good luck, resourcefulness, ability, and opportuity to make that dream come true; but for most of us, even the possibility seems increasingly remote. For the large majority of Americans, the possibility itself has never been more than a formal potentiality, and the chances of making it a material reality have been virtually nil. Maybe this is a jaundiced and cynical view (and we can surely debate the merits of that), but I am always impressed, as I interpret the economic development of this country through reading its social and intellectual history, by the fact that, on the whole, the rich have become richer and the poor have become poorer.

This assessment is not made lightly, nor is it without some awareness of the remarkable, gigantic strides we have made in scientific and technical achievement, in gross national product, and in attaining the highest standard of living in human history. But the ethical dilemmas of this society are not rooted in that kind of progress; the moral crises that confront us do not emerge from the risks attending our scientific accomplishments or the perils accompanying the promise of our technological triumphs. Our ethical dilemma is, first, that we cannot or will not agree upon a common set of values that take poverty seriously; second, that we have no firm consensus as to what is true and good and just; and, third, that we cannot any longer (if ever we could) assume that we share common notions of duties and rights. And our moral crises derive from that ethical heteronomy; because we cannot agree upon the principles of virtue, we are in conflict about the practice of virtue.

The problem of poverty has arisen and remained unsolved because of an idolatry; in this case, wealth and the power it brings are valued over persons and the varieties of human need. Were it not for our commitment and devotion to existing economic arrangements and institutions, novel ideas and novel ways of organizing and managing wealth and of eradicating poverty might emerge. Our great difficulty in conceiving new ideas and ways may only indicate the measure to which the old idolatry holds us captive. Poverty comes into being because of a distorted perspective on private property, the place of work, the use of wealth, and the relative value of men and machines. So, it is not intellectual stagnation, economic incapacity, or any similar impotence which accounts for the maintenance of poverty amid affluence, but only our bondage to this idol. Poverty is finally a human problem.

In 1969 Rodger Hurley published a remarkable book, *Poverty and Mental Retardation*, in which he documented the shocking extent to which poverty in this country cripples its victims both culturally and neurophysiologically. He commented specifically:

The most frightening instance of the over-representation of the Negro . . . is found in reports of the Eugenics Board of North Carolina. Over a period of thirty-seven years this Board has overseen the sterilization of 6,851 persons, some by means of castration. Not all of these individuals were sterilized for feeblemindedness; mental illness and until recently, epilepsy were also considered adequate reasons to subject individuals to this utter degradation. In the two-year period beginning July 1, 1964, 356 persons were sterilized: 124 were white, 228 were Negro, and four were Indian. In the previous two-year period, 507 persons were sterilized; 150 were white, 323 were Negro, and fourteen were Indian. There are approximately three whites to every Negro in the North Carolina population.[2]

In the United States in 1964, Hurley continued, the overall rate of infant mortality was 24.8 per one thousand births. When this figure, however, was broken down by color, the rate for nonwhite infants was 41.1 per thousand, almost twice the white rate. He also established that black children are far more likely than white children to receive poor prenatal care and are therefore more likely to be born prematurely. That, in turn, makes the black baby sixteen times more likely to die during the neonatal period (the first twenty-eight days), or if he survives he is ten times more likely to be brain damaged and mentally retarded. Hurley reinforced the claim of "poor prenatal care for the poor" by further statistics:

More than ten percent of all nonwhite mothers in this country in 1964 gave birth without a physician in attendance; this rate was more than twenty percent in several Southern states. . . . In general service delivery clinics . . . quantity must of necessity take precedence over quality. This observation should not be misunderstood as meaning that clinic service is tantamount to no service at all, but the quality of medical service one receives is directly related to the price one pays. For general service delivery the poor pay very little or nothing and, thus, they "definitely get second-rate medical care."

More recent data, cited at the Southern Rural Health Conference in October, 1976, have done nothing to dispute

2. Rodger Hurley, *Poverty and Mental Retardation* (New York: Random House, 1969), 45–46, 58–59, 62.

Hurley's fundamental assessment. A preliminary task force report on rural southern health showed that about half of the nation's poor live in the thirteen, largely rural southern states; that the death rate in the rural South is 22 percent higher than the national average; that the "infant mortality rate . . . is 65 percent higher for rural blacks than rural whites"; that doctors perpetuate racially segregated waiting rooms in some areas; and that, since the ability to pay for medical care is lower and the resources for medical care fewer, the rural South continues to be disadvantaged by biases in the system of health care delivery.[3]

The reasons for this situation in this country, at this time, are doubtless many and complex; but prominent among them is the notion that health care should be a monopoly of the medical profession. American medical professionals have achieved increasing affluence, a higher social status than any other group in our society, and virtually unchallenged control over the definition as well as the social and economic conditions of its work. And the result, according to Michael Michaelson, is that "health is no more a priority of the American health industry than safe, cheap, efficient, pollution-free transportation is priority of the American automobile industry."[4]

Among many similar studies, I have cited Hurley's to indicate why I choose to ignore statistical data here. Although his book is well documented and its conclusions are generally accepted, it has not made any significant difference in the areas it addressed. North Carolina legislators did recently remove epileptics from the list of those persons who were liable to be involuntarily sterilized on order by the state eugenics board, and I do not discount this step toward

3. *Washington Post*, October 11, 1976, A, 26.
4. Michael Michaelson, "The Coming Medical War," in Richard W. Wertz (ed.), *Readings on Ethical and Social Issues in Biomedicine* (Englewood Cliffs, N.J.: Prentice-Hall, 1973), 269–85.

a more just and humane society; but the evidence is compelling that this action was taken on medical rather than ethical grounds.

Although Hurley's book (and many others like it) is an important comment on a major social issue, it is, unfortunately, consigned to the oblivion reserved for such commentaries. This ought not to be surprising to those of us who read history; since the time of St. Augustine, if not that of Amos and Job, we have known that choices, for all their cognitive and discursive supports, are preeminently a function of will. Knowing this puts the recitation of "objective data" into perspective, because the preeminence of *voluntas* means that there is no such thing as an uninterpreted fact, that reason is always in the service of a higher affective loyalty, and that propositional knowledge is the public exhibition of an intensely personal and tacit commitment. Statistics, at least those which reflect the plight of the poor, perform this function for us. They show us that knowledge alone does not insure action.

For example, it is widely, if not devoutly, held that equal access to comprehensive medical service, irrespective of socioeconomic, geographic, or other boundaries, should be available to every American. Indeed, some consider it to be a basic right of citizens in this society. Yet there continues to be fundamental conflict, if not in the rhetoric then certainly in its pragmatic applications, between the rights of the medical practitioners to chart their own course without annoying intrusions from government or some other party and the rights of citizens to medical services.

Of course we all know certain individuals, both inside and outside the field of medicine, who dispute the principle of equal access; indeed, one physician has argued that doctors are like bakers in that "the only 'right' to the bread belongs to the baker, and . . . a claim by any other man to that right is unjustified and can be enforced only by violence or the threat of violence. . . . Medical care is neither a right nor a privilege: it is a service that is provided by doctors and others to people who wish to purchase it."[5] Just now it would probably be presumptuous, if not foolish, to predict where American medicine will go on this matter; but it is relatively easy to suppose that social security, medicaid, and medicare are the prelude to a national health service program of some sort. The form that this program will take depends, in large part, upon the answers to questions of professional and public prerogative.

No less widely held, but probably less generally disparaged, is the value of a close and personal relationship between patient and physician. That value is served by the patient's freedom to select a doctor whom he trusts and respects for his professional performance. And the obligation, certainly in Western medicine, of the physician to serve solely the interests of the patient is only one of many rubrics that reinforce the appropriateness of such a relationship. But difficulty occurs again precisely at the point of a conflict of loyalties between physician autonomy and patient participation.

I want to emphasize that this is a genuine difficulty, inasmuch as the physician *is* simultaneously an agent of the profession and doctor to an individual patient. Although these two roles might ideally coalesce, they do not always dovetail so neatly in actual practice. In a time of scarce resources it is particularly evident that a physician may be quickly impaled on the horns of this dilemma. He has a utilitarian obligation to do the greatest good for the greatest number, yet he must respond to a claim for special consideration by the individual patient for whom he is responsible. The issue of personalization versus professionalization is well worn but urgent.

Patient participation in medical decisions is yet another value extolled by both providers and consumers alike. The

5. Robert M. Sade, "Medical Care As a Right: A Refutation," *New England Journal of Medicine*, CCLXXXV (December 2, 1971), 1288–92.

advantages appear to be obvious and self-evident; but this relationship, too, is often frustrated by patient knowledge (or lack of it) about medical matters, together with the professional sovereignty which the physician retains concerning "his" patients. It may well be that American consumers are increasingly knowledgeable about individual illnesses and the practice of medicine, but this increase in information is not commensurate with either the power to alter the system or the expertise to intervene in a physician's decisions about diagnosis and treatment.

The abortion controversy has dramatically illustrated both the promise and the peril of patient participation in what are allegedly medical decisions; and it has simultaneously raised serious questions about the extent to which physicians are engaged in social, as distinguished from per se medical, interventions. It is being increasingly recognized that the delivery of health services "on demand" is not an unmixed blessing, that the strident rhetoric of radicals and liberals does threaten to convert the physician into a plumber, and that our self-deception by so-called medical indications has now given way to frank acknowledgement of the overriding personal and social dimensions of abortion (and, by extension, other interventions). These overriding dimensions, by their universality, promise to confuse all the old distinctions between elective and indicated procedures and, in turn, to make explicit and public what has been operative all along—namely, that medicine is a social institution and that sickness and health are social constructions. These facts do not necessarily call into radical question medicine as such or the particular ways in which we view illness and well being; but they do oblige us to take a serious look at the subjective valuations that ineluctably influence the denomination of certain conditions as disease and other conditions as health. On the basis of that serious look we must begin to reassess how and to whom the available health resources are distributed and employed.

Peter Schuck, who is director of the Washington, D.C., office of Consumers Union, recently described five dimensions of the current health care crisis. First, "Many consumers, particularly the inner-city poor and those in rural areas, lack access to primary health care services and particularly to services that could *prevent* illness."[6] The problem of the distribution of health care professionals is enormously complex; even so, the data indicates the nature of the problem. In 1974, for example, the ratio of physicians to population was 84:100,000 in South Dakota but 249:100,000 in New York. In the nation, the ratio has gone from 126:100,000 in 1930 to 174:100,000 in 1975, and is projected to be 196:100,000 in 1980. Second, "Consumers increasingly perceive a crisis in the quality of health care"; In terms of performance there appear to be significant variations among hospitals, clinics, and physicians. The result is that disproportionately poor or low quality care is sometimes the only care available.

Third, "Consumers perceive a crisis in health care costs," which last year (1975) rose 15 percent and are increasing 2½ times faster than the Consumer Price Index. In 1960 the nation's total health care expenditures were $25.9 billion, representing 5.2 percent of the GNP; in 1975 the bill was $110 billion, about 8 percent of the GNP. Consumers, particularly the poor, are concerned that there appears to be no end in sight to the ever-increasing inflationary spiral of health care costs. Fourth, a crisis "flows from the emerging configuration of health care services in America, principally the drastic decline in primary physicians (particularly general practitioners) and the corresponding growth in the specialities and sub-specialities." In the previous decade there was a decline from 59 to 41.5 primary physicians per 100,000 population; one of the unfortunate effects of this

6. Peter H. Schuck, "A Consumer's View of the Health Care System," in Laurence R. Tancredit (ed.), *Ethics of Health Care* (Washington, D.C.: National Academy of Sciences, 1974), 97–99.

decline is the diminution of low-cost preventive medicine. Fifth, a crisis "exists in the sense that the health level of the American public is quite low relative to that of other industrialized nations." Life expectancy among both men and women is lower, and infant mortality is far higher in the United States than in several other developed countries; and this is the case despite the fact that Americans, by comparison, spend far more per capita for health care. One can surely argue with these interpretations; indeed, it is the perpetual argument that maintains the *status quo ante* and prevents us from getting off dead center in the entire matter of health care for the poor.

A view of the problem from another perspective will underscore the human dimension that overrides and permeates any morally sensitive consideration of poverty as a problem for medical care systems and medical professionals. Even the casual visitor to an outpatient clinic can experience the awful sense of outrage and terror that is the companion of radical dependency. Jonathan Kozol gives a powerful account of such an experience:

Boston, Blue Hill Avenue, Ten days Before Christmas: A child falls down in the middle of Grove Hall. She is epileptic, but her sickness either has not been diagnosed or else (more probable) it has been diagnosed, but never treated. Tall and thin, fourteen years old, she is intense and sober, devastated but unhating. Her life is a staccato sequence of *grand mal* convulsions: no money, no assistance, no advice on how to get a refill of inexpensive script for more Dilantin and more phenobarbital.

This night, she comes downstairs into the office where I work within the coat-room underneath the church-stairs of a Free School: standing there and asking me please if I would close the door and hold her head within my arms because she knows that she is going to have an epileptic seizure; and closing the door and sitting down upon the cold cement while she lies down and places her head within my arms and starts to shudder violently and moves about so that I scarcely can protect her wracked and thin young body from the cement wall and from the concrete floor; and seeing her mouth writhe up with pain and spittle, and feeling her thrash about a second time and now a third; and, in between, the terror closing in upon her as in a child's bad dream that you can't get out of, and watching her then, and wondering what she undergoes; and later seeing her, exhausted, sleeping there, right in my arms, as at the end of long ordeal, all passion in her spent; then taking her out into my car and driving with her to the City Hospital while she, as epileptics very often feel, keeps saying that she is going to have another seizure; and slamming on the brakes and walking with her in the back door where they receive out-patient cases, and being confronted on this winter night at nine p.m. in Boston in the year of 1965 with a scene that comes from Dante's Purgatory: dozens and dozens of poor white, black and Puerto Rican people, infants and mothers, old men, alcoholics, men with hands wrapped up in gauze, and aged people trembling, infants trembling with fever; one hostile woman in white uniform behind the table telling us, out of a face made, it seems, of clay, that we should fill an application out, some sort of form, a small white sheet, then sit out in the hallways since the waiting room is full; and then to try to say this child has just had several seizures in a row and needs treatment, and do we need to do the form; and yes, of course you need to do the form and wait your turn and not think you have any special right to come ahead of someone else who has been sitting here before you. Two hours and four seizures later, you get up and go in and shout in her cold eyes and walk right by and grab an intern by the arm and tell him to come out and be a doctor to an epileptic child sitting like a damp rag in the hallway; and he comes out, and in two minutes gives this child an injection that arrests the seizures and sedates her, then writes the script for more Dilantin and for phenobarbital and shakes his head and says to you that it's a damn shame: "Nobody needs to have an epileptic seizure in this day and age. . . . Nobody but a poor black nigger," says the intern in a sudden instant of that rage that truth and decency create. He nearly cries, and in his eyes you see a kind of burning pain that tells you that he is a good man somehow, deep-down, some place where it isn't all cold stone, clean surgery and antiseptic reason: "Nobody but a poor black nigger needs to have an epileptic seizure anymore." So you take her home and you go back to the church, down to your office underneath the stairs, and look at the floor, and listen to the silence, and you are twenty-eight years old, and you begin to cry; you cry for horror of what that young girl has just been through; and you long not to believe that this can be the city that you really live in. You fight

very hard to lock up that idea because it threatens all the things
that you have wanted to believe for so long; so you sit alone a
while and you try to lock these bitter passions into secret spaces of
your self-control. You try to decontaminate your anger and to organize your rage; but you can't do it this time; you just can't build
that barrier of logical control a second time. . . . *Grand mal,* you
think to yourself, means a great evil. [7]

I am clearly committed to reshaping the system of health
care delivery in this society to provide a larger measure of
medical and surgical benefit to the oppressed poor among us
who cannot obtain it under the present arrangement; I am
revolted and horrified that a profession committed to caring
for the hurts and illnesses of people should place institutional protocols or professional reward or whatever else before that obligation. Simultaneously I support the very institutions and systems that create this disaster; I want my
wife and daughters to see the best gynecologist, my son to
have the best pediatric care available, and all of us to be
covered by a prepaid medical and hospital plan. I pay the
bill for these services with a sense of grudging and gratitude,
while I find unconscionable the denial of these same services to people who are too poor to pay for them. To compound the irony, I am paid by the university to give courses
on medical ethics and by hospitals and medical schools to
lecture on these subjects.

I am driven by neither a neurotic need for innocence nor
a revolutionary's demand for self-justification. If I can
choose the circumstance, I do not object to placing myself
and my family in a vulnerable position. The critical factor
in this moral problem has been my freedom to choose those
circumstances I would otherwise find distasteful or unacceptable. That is a luxury, however relative, of which the
poor are by definition deprived. The resulting inequity may
be no less that they are denied that choice than that they are
in large measure the patients of crowded inner city clinics,

7. Jonathan Kozol, *The Night Is Dark and I Am Far From Home* (Boston:
Houghton Mifflin, 1975), 59–61.

where they receive marginal services from staff members willing to trade off the obligation to do this work for the promise of more tolerable and attractive futures.

Justice, in its fundamental moral sense, means fairness in terms of giving what is deserved, whether affirming or denying. Distributive justice attempts to supply a person or group with its due proportion of goods, services, or opportunities. Conversely, retributive justice endeavors to deprive a person or group of the proportion that is not due. Justice is, therefore, calculating; it measures what shall be given or what shall be withheld. But it is also proportional, that is, it calculates not only what shall be given or taken away but also how much; to this extent, justice intends to be righteous. Operational justice, by definition, ineluctably entails the exercise of power as the effective mechanism for giving or taking away according to proportional deserts. And that is why, in any discussion of distributive justice and American health care, the issue of power is unavoidable. Without power there can be no justice, because justice is the form that power actualizes in the conflict between the haves and the have-nots, between claim and counterclaim.

The problem of health care for the poor is so insidious and thoroughgoing that we have not yet clearly sorted out all of its aspects. But I know that there will be no answer if we deny the problem. The difficulties of examining the problem are compounded by our capacity for self-deception and clever but accommodating strategies, which is probably exceeded only by our aptitude for oppression. So a beginning will probably have been made when we appreciate that the presence of the oppressed poor in the struggle for their liberation is not optional but essential.

Morality and Foreign Policy

JOHN C. BENNETT

FOR MANY reasons morality often seems a stranger in the area of foreign policy. I doubt if there is any aspect of public life in which it is more difficult to apply the moral standards we generally take for granted. In fact, some people assume that we must have a double standard which separates the morality we seek to realize in most areas of life from the criteria that should guide foreign policy, particularly the criteria related to some concept of national necessity, of amoral realpolitik. I recognize the depth of the problem, but I refuse to separate the morality of states in international relations from the morality that should guide us in our own national life. A government is more limited than an individual; it is a trustee for a nation. There should be continuous interaction between our striving for the good both in foreign policy and in other areas that may be less recalcitrant.

Some reasons why foreign policy is so difficult from a moral standpoint follow:

1. The moral relations between people across national boundaries are often quite thin. This is not equally so across all boundaries, but it is the case when people differ in culture, language, ideology, or the conditions of their lives. It is difficult for Americans to imagine themselves in the place of people in Bangladesh or Cuba. We assign false or one-sided stereotypes to people in many other nations. Also, be-

tween some nations there is a history of hostility. This need not go on forever.

2. Nations feel insecure, even feel that their existence is threatened in this dangerous world. Great powers feel this as keenly as small nations do, though in a different way, because each of them is such a potential threat to the other. No amount of armament makes our own country feel secure. It is not quite true that the world of nations is, as Thomas Hobbes said of life in general, "a war of every man against every man"; but there is no system of collective security that enables nations to feel safe.[1] The moral importance of this is that it is easy for a nation to ignore its conscience and justify almost any means toward attaining national security.

3. So much of the world's political history depicts the persistence of evil, tragedies, vicious circles of conflict between nations. There have always been deep moral dilemmas and choices of lesser evils. The situation is often so complex that no obvious moral formulas fit it. Rules are in conflict. The present time reveals great contrasts, because it could be regarded as the most humanitarian of all periods and also as the period in which the cruelest deeds have been perpetrated on a large scale. I see this period as one of struggle between these opposites—a struggle of peace and humane societies against the threat of massive technological destruction and the reality of tyranny, terror, and torture. In taking account of real obstacles, however, I want to avoid implying that we are hopelessly entrapped by the past and that there can be no new occurrences.

4. There is a dilution of responsibility in the making of foreign policy in a democracy. Although this is better than the opposite situation in which foreign policy is made in secret by authoritarian rulers, it has its own moral problems.

1. Thomas Hobbes, *Leviathon, or the Matter, Forme, and Power of a Commonwealth, Ecclesiasticall and Civil*, ed. Michael Oakeshott (Oxford, England: Basil Blackwell, 1946 [1651], 83.

The policy makers often see themselves limited by public opinion or by an organized minority chiefly in one party; consequently, they pass the buck to the public. But much of the public assumes that the policy makers are on the spot and should know best, and thus it passes the buck to them. This process is illustrated in the development of policy toward Communist China during the sixties. Political leaders were intimidated by the public on the China issue and were inclined to postpone leadership on this controversial issue until after the next election. Meanwhile, public opinion on the subject began to change, and finally it was put to the test by a most unlikely person, Richard Nixon. His reopening of relations with China became the one thing for which he was given high marks.

5. A fifth difficulty is well stated in some startling words of Reinhold Niebuhr: "Patriotism transmutes individual unselfishness into national egoism."[2] Since I do not want to leave patriotism to the chauvinists, I would prefer to call it *nationalism* (though even nationalism is a good in nations seeking to achieve unity). The point is true enough. The moral impulses of the individual are often fully satisfied by his or her national loyalty, and the test of good character may be what one does for his countryfolk. The loyalty and the goodness of the citizens may be used by the nation in the pursuit of egoistic ends, which are largely and easily hidden by a nation's claiming the sanction of universal ideals or a universal religion. This leads Niebuhr also to say that "perhaps the most significant moral characteristic of a nation is its hypocrisy."[3] I do not believe that we should take either of the above sentences from Niebuhr as being always true, but they do suggest the moral vulnerability of nations, their people, and their governments.

6. A less obvious and more puzzling difficulty exists.

2. Reinhold Niebuhr, *Moral Man and Immoral Society* (New York: Scribner and Sons, 1932), 91.
3. *Ibid.*, 95.

When nations emphasize that they are serving high moral goals, they may become crusaders for those goals and therefore more unrestrained, destructive, and unable to accept the accommodations necessary for living together or bringing a way to an end. In 1971 Arthur Schlesinger, Jr., published an article in *Harpers Magazine* with the startling title, "The Necessary Amorality of Foreign Affairs." He says, "The compulsion to see foreign affairs in moral terms may have, with the noblest of intentions, the most ghastly consequences."[4]

Hans Morgenthau, the dean of political scientists concerned about foreign policy, has greatly emphasized this idea. He says, "What is good for the crusading nation is by definition good for all mankind, and, if the rest of mankind refuses to accept such claims to universal recognition, it must be converted by fire and sword."[5] Many of us believe that this course of action accounts for part of the story, especially the early part, of our war in Indo-China. After 1967 we were no longer fighting for a cause but fighting to avoid our own defeat and loss of credibility.

George Kennan, another expert on foreign policy, emphasizes the same danger. His fear is that we will be self-righteous and pretentious in assuming that we know what is good for other nations. He calls for national humility and self-restraint, a highly moral emphasis.[6] The word *moralism* is often thrown around when this kind of consideration is put forward. Moralism generally refers to something that is disapproved, morality to something that is approved. What is moralism? Generally it seems to mean the tendency to make one moral value absolute while neglecting others and to announce one's position about this in a

4. Arthur Schlesinger, Jr., "The Necessary Amorality of Foreign Affairs," *Harpers Magazine*, CCXLIII (August, 1971), 72–77.
5. Hans Morgenthau, *In Defense of the National Interest* (New York: Alfred Knopf, 1951), 37.
6. George F. Kennan, *Realities of American Foreign Policy* (Princeton, N.J.: Princeton University Press, 1954), 98–99.

self-righteous tone of voice. Those who warn most against moralism or against the dangers of moral crusading have their own way of affirming the role of morality in foreign policy.

Three considerations that reflect a sensitive, universal, and humane morality in foreign policy are (1) motives, attitudes, and intentions regarding those who are likely to pay the price for policies—the melding of moral concern and perception is central; (2) the criteria for choosing short range and long range goals; (3) the moral limits to means that are used.

The best motives of policy makers and of citizens who endorse or oppose policy are not enough. Secretary of State Cyrus Vance, in his testimony before the Senate committee at the time of his confirmation in 1977, made a very important statement about American policy in Vietnam. He said, "In the light of hindsight I believe it was a mistake to have intervened in Vietnam" and "U.S. involvement was not based upon evil motives but on misjudgments and mistakes as we went along." I believe that both statements are true. The persons who were originally responsible for policy thought that they were preserving freedom and self-determination in South Vietnam and that our policy was a contribution to world order. The status of good motives may be questioned when people persist in a mistake for many years, long after its disastrous consequences have been revealed. To what extent have they, after being so long identified with a policy, acquired a vested interest in it and become unable to reject it?

Policy makers failed to perceive the full human consequences of what the policy was doing to people in Indo-China and in this country, especially the sons of the minorities and the poor, who bore so much of the burden. Robert McNamara was one of the major architects of American policy in Indo-China, and he did a great deal to sell it to the American people. By May, 1967, however, he had begun to change, and he sent a remarkable memorandum to President Lyndon B. Johnson that included the following statement: "The picture of the world's greatest superpower killing or seriously injuring 1,000 noncombatants a week while trying to pound a tiny backward nation into submission on an issue whose merits are hotly disputed, is not a pretty one. It could conceivably produce a costly distortion in the American national consciousness and in the world image of the U.S., especially if the damage to North Vietnam is complete enough to be 'successful.' " [7]

One indication that McNamara's change in perception had not gone far enough is in his reference to Vietnam as a "tiny backward nation." It was backward in some respects (air power, for example). But that statement reflected a tendency to have contempt for people who were little known or understood and whose problems we thought we could solve. That defect in perception underlies so many things that nations do to each other. People toward whom we have that attitude seem to us to be more expendable than others; we tell ourselves that they do not value human life as much as we do. To achieve morality we must begin with good motives, but these need to be combined with other subjective elements: sensitivity, imagination, perception.

In a famous speech at Amherst College in 1964, Dean Acheson stated quite well the declared objectives of American foreign policy since World War II. He said, "The end sought by our foreign policy, the purpose for which we carry on relations with foreign states, is, (as I have said) to preserve and foster an environment in which free societies may exist and flourish." I quote from this speech because Acheson's main emphasis was to criticize people who think of foreign policy in terms of morality. Yet the objective, as he stated it, is a moral objective. No American statesman can

7. Neil Sheehan, Hendrick Smith, E. W. Kenworthy, and Fox Butterfield, *The Pentagon Papers As Published by the New York Times* (New York: Bantam Books, 1971), 580.

speak about foreign policy without assuring our people, usually with a good deal of moralizing rhetoric, that it does have moral objectives.

Next to these objectives and very close to them in importance for statesmen in recent times has been the prevention of nuclear war. This is the main purpose of detente, and it justifies detente against all of its critics.

The objectives of American foreign policy have been too one-sided. Not enough is said about justice. Though we use the words "liberty and justice for all," a defect in the conventional American scale of values reveals our tendency to put liberty far above justice. In our own society we rationalize this by assuming that justice will be a by-product of the freedom of free enterprise, but it has not worked out that way for 25 million or more of our people. Equality of opportunity is unreal if inequalities in conditions are extreme.

In international affairs we have emphasized free societies and have tried to prevent revolutionary changes that have as their goal economic justice for a nation as a whole. We did all that we could until recently to undermine or thwart the revolution in China, which lacks the freedoms of our Bill of Rights but has experienced great achievements in overcoming massive poverty. In Latin America we have consistently opposed revolutions from the left, beginning with Cuba. Zbigniew Brzezinski, President Jimmy Carter's adviser, in a 1976 article, shows that the United States is becoming isolated because it puts freedom so high above all other values, whereas most of humanity puts equality above freedom.[8] I suggest that we put, not equality, but justice that is always under the pull of equality on the same level with freedom; it would transform our foreign policy. We cannot expect freedom where the dominant realities are poverty and hunger.

There is a great irony about all of this. For all of our de-

8. Zbigniew Brzezinski, "America in a Hostile World," *Foreign Policy*, XXIII (Summer, 1976), 65–97.

clared support of free societies we seem so often to favor governments that care nothing about either freedom or justice, that deal brutally with political dissent and do very little for 80 percent of their people; Brazil, Chile, South Vietnam, and South Korea are examples. In practice we have had two criteria by which to determine policy in relation to Third World nations—whether they are anti-Communist and whether they are receptive to American business. Our foreign policy would rise to a higher moral level if we were to judge it rigorously by the degree to which it serves both freedom and justice. This means putting our minds on the problems of world poverty and hunger and on the need to take long steps toward economic justice between nations.

Among other objectives, one of which is to act as a faithful trustee of the global environment for the sake of future generations, is the prevention of much more than nuclear war. Today there must be a heavier burden of proof on all use of military force among nations and, for us especially, on the military intervention by our government in the internal conflicts of other nations. We should allow other nations to have their own revolutions.

Prevention of particular wars is not enough. The emphasis should also be on positive peacemaking, on the use and strengthening of multilateral institutions. Charles Yost, who was deputy representative of the U.S. from 1961 through 1966 and the ambassador to the United Nations from 1969 to 1971, has said that "neither President Johnson nor President Nixon had any real respect for the United Nations." [9] He was in a good position to know. There is some hope in the fact that Cyrus Vance had said that he would make much use of the United Nations.

Regarding the moral limits to the means we use, we have

9. Charles Yost, *The Conduct and Misconduct of Foreign Affairs* (New York: Random House, 1972), 580.

bitter moral dilemmas. I am sure that we would all say that not everything is morally permitted, whatever the goal; but where do we draw the line? There was great moral revulsion when it was discovered that the Central Intelligence Agency had been involved in plots to assassinate Fidel Castro and other foreign leaders. We can draw the line at assassination as a method of conducting the relations between states. I found myself approving the attempt by some Germans whom I admired very much, including Dietrich Bonhoeffer, to assassinate Adolf Hitler. It is not enough to say that Castro is no Hitler. We should also say that the plot against Hitler was an inside German act of rebellion and that such rebellions may be justified in extreme cases of oppression, unless one is an absolute pacifist. When assassination takes place as an episode in foreign policy, there is no way of containing the spreading mistrust that would be created. Nothing could do more to poison relationships. Charles James Fox, one of the greatest friends of the American colonies in Britain, when he was British foreign minister in 1806, set a good example for the CIA. When someone came to him and offered to assassinate Napoleon, with whom his country was at war, Fox was horrified. He had the man arrested and notified the French foreign minister.

The Second Vatican Council stated a principle that has had a high place in the Western moral tradition of setting limits. It said, "Any act of war aimed indiscriminately at the destruction of entire cities or extensive areas along with their population is a crime against God and man himself."[10] The statement had been watered down, because some American bishops did not want the council to condemn explicitly a policy of nuclear deterrence. But our system of deterrence raises a profound problem. The missiles of the United States

10. "Pastoral Constitution on the Modern World," par. 80 in Walter M. Abbott (ed.), *The Documents of Vatican II* (New York: Herder and Herder, 1966), 294.

and the Soviet Union are aimed indiscriminately at the destruction of entire cities. Proposals that this strategy be changed and that missiles be aimed at the missile sites or armed forces of the potential adversary are criticized, because this strategy is believed to be more threatening, suggesting a "first strike" capability, and more likely to bring about the war in which the missles would be used. This is a horrendous moral issue. In the short run, the strategy of deterrence may prevent nuclear war. But in the long run, not only is this very doubtful, but the strategy that makes the people of a nation accustomed to the idea of being potential destroyers of populations is itself morally corrupting. How long can we live with it? Morally, it becomes necessary to find other means both in terms of disarmament, or at least the radical reduction of armaments, and in terms of reconciliation between the powers that may destroy not only each other but all the innocent bystanders caught in the cross fire.

I have referred to Hans Morgenthau as an expert in international affairs who is usually seen as playing down the moral factor in foreign policy. But he draws limits to means. In a 1970 speech in New York, after the My Lai massacre in Vietnam had caused moral revulsion in our country, he said we should have known that in a war in Indo-China we would become guilty of intolerable immorality and, therefore, we should not have become involved in the first place. Coming from him, this statement was more remarkable than it would have been coming from me. Moral limits? In a more generalized way I think that we should draw the limits this side of covert operations to overturn foreign governments. We should draw them this side of a counter-revolutionary policy that attempts to keep the lid on primarily indigenous attempts to overcome oppressive governments and economic institutions with which our government and our corporations may have been too comfortable. In saying these things I realize that borderline situations exist and that it is difficult to be in this peaceful place and set forth absolute laws for application to all known or unknown situations.

Yet this thinking about limits in advance is essential. It should put a very heavy burden of proof on all who may find reasons to say that any future situation should be treated as an exception. There may be few absolute laws, but there are secure moral landmarks. And these can be guides and warnings. There are great complexities and tragic dilemmas, but we need not consign foreign policy to a wilderness without moral signs.

In recent months the relation of American foreign policy to our government's support of human rights around the world has received special emphasis. In fact people often seem to assume that foreign policy begins to have a moral aspect only when human rights are involved. This is a great error. The concern to prevent war is as highly moral as the support of human rights. Indeed it is doubtful whether the survivors of a nuclear war would have many such rights. The concern about justice between nations has great moral importance. This does not make light of the emphasis on human rights but rather puts it in the context of a broader moral commitment.

It is very desirable for our nation, our government, and our president, who is a new voice among the nations, to make very clear the commitment of the American people to human rights as expressed in our Bill of Rights. It should be recognized that the American concern for the rights of individual expression is often presented in a one-sided way. The Universal Declaration of Human Rights, to which both the United States and the Soviet Union are committed, includes the rights of individual expression that are so familiar to us and social rights such as the right to work, to protection against unemployment, and to medical care. Nations should be judged both by their record regarding individual rights as Americans usually understand them and by their record regarding social justice among their people.

The American role in relation to the rights of the individual needs to be seen in the light of one regrettable fact—people in most countries today live under authoritarian governments, and for such governments the freedom of the individual does not have a very high priority. These are not all totalitarian governments, and there is a wide spectrum among them concerning various forms of personal freedom. The causes of this authoritarian trend need to be understood. Nations with no previous experience of self-government, let alone of democratic government, often have the task of establishing order and national unity when the odds are against both. They also have the task of overcoming in a few years the results of generations or centuries of economic stagnation and poverty, if life is to be tolerable for their people. Some of them have been through violent revolutions, and remnants of the old order are objects of deep resentment because of former oppression and threats to the stability of the new order. Sinful abuse of power is very much present, but this is combined with all the problems of managing a rapidly changing nation that faces enormous handicaps. Consider the very wise words of Abraham Lincoln: "Must a government, of necessity, be too strong for the liberties of its own people, or too weak to maintain its own existence?" (from a message to Congress in special session, July 4, 1861). We might add, or too weak to deal with extraordinarily difficult problems that are fateful for the viability of the nation.

Contrast our own origin as a nation. We had behind us a remarkable experience of self-government in the colonies and in British history. We had great resources, an open frontier, a small population, and, at least among white people, no mass poverty. Moreover most of the opponents of our revolution lived three thousand miles away, and their opposition was halfhearted. Few nations that have had revolutions in our time have had such luck. The establishment of our republic as a new nation was a great achievement, but the circumstances were most favorable and they have been favorable for us as a nation ever since. This situation leads me to call for carefulness and restraint regarding our temptation to preach to most of the human race from a fortunate pulpit, often with a one-sided sense of moral priorities.

We need to find ways of testifying to our convictions that avoid a self-righteous stance. We should encourage the widest multilateral protest possible against particular atrocities such as torture or long imprisonment without trial. Internationally, artists, scientists, jurists, and churches can do a great deal to defend human rights against the arbitrary and cruel power of governments. Private organizations such as Amnesty International have an extremely important role. In Latin America today the Roman Catholic Church is the most powerful defender of human rights; in South Korea this is true of both Protestant and Catholic churches.

Another consideration needs emphasis. The support of human rights by our government has been appallingly inconsistent. We have been very tolerant of the denials of human rights by many rightist regimes. The present administration is trying to break with the past in this respect and has begun to reduce or to deny aid to some Latin American nations because of their record on human rights. Brazil, which has been one of the nations most favored by our government as a bastion of capitalism, has become alienated from us because our State Department has criticized its policies of repression and torture. The Ford-Kissinger administration had already been critical of the junta in Chile for this same reason. Yet, so many anti-Communist nations with bad human rights records, such as South Korea, Iran, the Philippines, and Indonesia, are in our camp, and little or no action is taken against them. In view of these inconsistencies the concentration on the treatment of dissidents in the Soviet Union raises serious questions. I do not mean that our leaders should be silent about the repression in the Soviet Union, but I have in mind a matter of relative emphasis. Also, what we do in relation to internal policies in the Soviet Union and in eastern European countries may be counterproductive. There are two ways in which this may be the case. The one most often stressed is that our actions may lead to an increase of repression, especially for dissidents who are not widely known. Perhaps more important is the danger that the more liberal elements in Communist nations and in Communist parties in western Europe may be handicapped if their own protests are linked with American initiatives and labeled as imperialistic and anti-Communist.

Much can be done for human rights by emphasizing the great diversity among Communist regimes and parties. As long ago as 1961 Brzezinski called attention to the effect of diversity among Communist nations, saying that it meant "a gradual relativization of the formerly absolutistic ideology." [11] In the long run this is the kind of development most favorable to flexibility and freedom. For the most part American policy has been to drive all nations or parties that are Marxist or Communist into the same corner. We have made an exception in regard to the rift between China and the Soviet Union and in the cases of Yugoslavia and, more recently, Rumania. But the trend has been the other way in our dealings with Cuba, Vietnam, Chile, Angola, and the Communist parties in western Europe. As I have said, there seems to be a change on the way under the Carter administration.

It is helpful to see Communist regimes and parties on a spectrum, with Cambodia and North Korea, the two most closed Communist societies, at one end, Yugoslavia, Hun-

11. Zbigniew Brzezinski, "Challenge of Change in the Soviet Bloc," *Foreign Affairs*, XXXIX (April, 1961) 442.

gary, and Poland at the other end, and the Communist parties in western Europe, especially in Italy, out beyond them. There is today great ferment in the whole world of Communists, and out of this may come greater respect for human rights than anything we can do. Above all, we should not do anything that has the effect of driving Communist nations or parties together.

Marshall Shulman, a Harvard University professor, one of the chief experts on the Soviet Union, and a member of the State Department, recently wrote the following about prospects for human rights in the Soviet Union: "We cannot predict which way the Soviet system will evolve in the future. But it seems reasonable to believe that the easing of repression is more likely to come from evolutionary forces within that society under prolonged conditions of reduced international tension than from external demands for change and the siege mentality they would enforce." [12]

It is a mistake to assume that the best way of being moral is to engage in a one-sided crusade for our form of individualistic human rights. These are an essential part of the person's freedom, which is rightly precious to us, and we should affirm them in our own national life and in what we stand for in the world. But it is also a moral responsibility to reduce tensions between the nuclear giants and to prevent war between them. The institutions of freedom would not be likely to survive such a war, even in our own country. It is a moral responsibility to help nations that are struggling with problems of poverty and to seek greater economic justice between peoples. When we discuss morality and foreign policy, let us remember the many-sidedness of morality.

12. Marshall Shulman, "On Learning to Live with Authoritarian Regimes," *Foreign Affairs*, LV (January, 1977), 334.

Meditations on Institutions

DONALD W. SHRIVER, JR.

THIS meditation concerns the variety of institutions and disciplines represented in any large city and university and the issues of public policy that transcend our individual specialities or institutions. The subject of institutions, disciplines, and public policy is perceptively expounded by Sir Geoffrey Vickers. He has served as an administrator in various British government agencies and has a good theoretical mind and an understanding of the generalist nature of administration. In one of his books he says that he really feels out of step with most academics and other specialists in the world. He feels like the dog who goes around eating the crumbs under everyone else's table, and he goes on to say that "in these days when the rich in knowledge eat at such separate tables, only the dogs have a chance at a balanced diet." [1] I'm not sure that those of us who eat crumbs from the other tables are eating a balanced diet. There should, however, be a structured chance for us to do so. As an ethicist I make peace with the fact that ethics in our society is necessarily a very general topic. In his *Ethics*, Aristotle remarks that it is difficult in the field of ethics to be accounted an expert, because everyone thinks he knows something about ethics. And in this, Aristotle was exactly right. Ethics

1. Geoffrey Vickers, *The Art of Judgment* (New York: Basic Books, 1965), 11.

is and should be a subject of public knowledge and public debate.

There is not an institution head, a department chairman, a bank president, or pastor of a church who does not know that once you are the person visibly or invisibly in charge of an institution, your vision constricts to that institution on a daily basis. If there is a single master rule painted in invisible ink over the top of my own office door, it is "Be sure this institution survives." In these days of budgetary crises, that is no minor rule. Institutions turn out to be more fragile than many of us were raised to think. It turns out that banks *can* fail. It turns out too that banks are businesses that have to promote their public image through advertising and friendly services. At any rate, that rule deserves some criticism. It is not a very ethical maxim and may be revised to read, "Be sure that your institution *deserves* to survive." That is a much more difficult thought to reckon with.

By what measure does any institution deserve to survive? In my most sober moments the measure I choose is public service. René Williamson calls attention to the fact that the term *public servant* is a quiet gift of Christianity to Western politics. [2] Our politicians like to call themselves public servants even when they are in the process of swindling the public. The ideal situation would be for all our politicians truly to regard their public service as a ministry. These days I have to remind academic theological colleagues that the word *administration* has in it *ministry*. This word should be a lot more honorable in academic circles than it is. In my meaner moments as an administrator I have to say that if I weren't around, the faculty wouldn't be around much longer. That is the economic truth of the matter.

But the more ethical observation about our institutions is that they are poorly structured for asking, answering, and

2. René de Visme Williamson, *Independence and Involvement: A Christian Reorientation in Political Science* (Baton Rouge: Louisiana State University Press, 1964), 201.

acting on questions of the "public interest." They tend not to be servants of the "general welfare." That principle dawned on me personally in connection with my ten years of service at North Carolina State University. Most of my training was on the liberal arts side of the American university establishment, at Davidson College, Union Seminary, Yale, and Harvard. I did not really know what a land-grant school was when I returned to North Carolina in 1962. I discovered that, however you analyze the twentieth-century economic development of the South, the land-grant university plays a prominent role. But during my tour of duty at such a university I discovered few colleagues in the technologies who were good at identifying the relationship between what I knew best and what they knew best. I was teaching a class in the social studies department, one of those "service departments" that puts the icing of social science on the cake of engineering studies. Engineering students were not very patient with the things we studied in that course. The reality of poverty, for example, was beginning to dawn on American consciences in the early 1960s. One day I made the statement that the building of a highway through the middle of a city is a very important social act, not simply an engineering act. Several civil engineering students in the class look astonished. We spent the rest of that hour trying to imagine what happens to a hundred families in a ghetto when their homes are smashed by bulldozers. We tried to relate that to middle-class people whose trip downtown was made ten minutes faster by the highway.

A more powerful contact with interdisciplinary studies was my whole experience of the Vietnam war, through the students on that university campus. One evening in 1967 or 1968, when things were really getting hot in Vietnam, Senator William Fulbright was on television quizzing experts about the war. And Fulbright, a person at the very center of foreign affairs in this country, was asking questions about the Vietnam war exactly like my questions. I felt let down. I was in the same position that Peter Berger describes in his book *The Precarious Vision*. [3] He says we all grow up under the illusion that there is "somebody who knows." There must be somebody who knows because we do not know. Then comes that shattering moment in which we find out that "everybody is as much in the dark as we are." That can be a very poignant moment in the development of science.

The presupposition of science is not so much knowledge as ignorance, and the identification of ignorance is itself an important bit of knowledge. In this sense, the Vietnam war was subject to a massive failure of science. At least three kinds of failure are evident. First, there was a failure of academic analysis of the war. Probably in someone's books of political science or in someone's university, there were academics who were subjecting the war to a thorough examination from a political point of view. But if they were, they failed to communicate their findings to the right places, the right pressure points, soon enough. Second, the Vietnam war was a failure of our national politicians, those who are supposed to protect our national self-interest. Fulbright himself seemed unable to articulate our national self-interest in the war. What was worth the deaths of fifty thousand Americans? The nation finally woke up to the fact that, regarding our national self-interest in Vietnam, the emperor had very few clothes. Politicians should have known that and taught us that earlier. Third, we in the institution of the church and discipline of ethics failed to be morally discriminating. We saw that war as a continuation of World War II. We realized too late that the cost of protecting freedom was not going to be worth it, that the cost of protecting a village was going to be identical with the cost of

3. Peter Berger, *The Precarious Vision* (Garden City, N.Y.: Doubleday, 1961,) 83–84.

destroying it. I came to understand that even more pragmatically in response to the emerging issue of environmentalism in the late sixties and early seventies.

I was again thrown into an interdisciplinary exploration when I became one of three persons teaching the first environmental course at NC State. Our different backgrounds represented training in law and history, biological science, and ethics. Our concern for ecology, the science of our surroundings, was the beginning of an encounter with the interconnectedness of everything in the world, in practical as well as theoretical ways. Human life can be compared to a bowl of spaghetti; you wiggle it on one side and something on the other side moves. The scientific task in ecology is to trace interactions across that bowl of spaghetti. We might change the image of the earth that has come into our consciousness in recent years as a result of photography from the moon. Kenneth Boulding said he considers that photograph of the earth swimming in its sea of darkness and swirling clouds against the blue green background of endless space to be a depiction of one of the great cultural events of our time. I believe the same. Indeed, I would have to confess to a kind of blasphemous but irresistible identification with the thought of the New Testament—how God loves the world. Emotionally and ideographically for me, the idea of loving a world so lovely and precious becomes more real in terms of that photograph. That double thought, of our power both to photograph the world and to love it, is the agony of our time. We suffer from a disjoining of our love of power and power to love. How will we get those two together?

I can conclude this first meditation by observing how the interconnectedness of all our intellectual perspectives and our attempts to act in the public realm come to focus in the problems of technological change, public policy, and urban planning. As Max Stackhouse suggests, the city is in some ways man's most magnificent, large-scale artifact, its largest empirical project.[4] A city is a cameo of that global environment wherein one part affects almost all the other parts. The moral question that cities and ecosystems pose can be stated thus: How shall we learn to love our neighbors as persons like ourselves, including our neighbors whom we do not see very easily and whom we cannot see because they are our neighbors of fifty and a hundred years into the future? Answers to questions like that will require input from the leaders of at least four institutions—the land-grant university, government, the business corporation, and the Church. In conclusion, I offer thoughts on each of these four.

First, the charter of the land-grant university derived from one of the most creative acts of the federal government, the Morrell Act, in a year (1863) when it was engaged in a lot of destructive acts. The president of Michigan State University said in a speech some years ago that the land-grant philosophy is one major contribution of American higher education to the philosophy of higher education in the world. In contrast to the Universities of Virginia, the Harvards, and the Oxfords of this world, the land-grant university was born as technology and science were beginning to arise on the horizon of contemporary society in the midst of frontier America. The land-grant university built on the idea that it is possible to combine the teaching of knowledge from the past with the discovery of new knowledge and research and to provide the service of all that knowledge to a broad public. Teaching, research, and extension form the land-grant combination. What does the combination mean in the 1970s? I am not certain, but surely a charter like that needs perpetual updating, especially on the side of public service. The various publics of the land-grant university,

4. Max Stackhouse, *Ethics and The Urban Ethos* (Boston: Beacon Press, 1972), 1.

like those of other institutions in our society, are subject to the kind of selective attention that the squeaky wheel always gets. If the wheel wants to squeak louder in our society, it usually has to have some form of either political power or economic power, or preferably both. What would the Louisiana State University political science department discover if it studied its last thirty years of agricultural research efforts and plotted the pattern of those who benefited from the research in relation to their economic and political position in Louisiana? I have no empirical knowledge of Louisiana to suggest that the answer would be embarrassing. I do have some knowledge of North Carolina, however. In that state, the poor farmer did not get much service from some of the agricultural extension services sponsored through North Carolina State University.[5] The large farmers, some of them members of the legislature, easily tapped into that intellectual service in ways that all of us know only too well. Ethics enters into the choice of research projects and the financing of them. Legislators need to be tested on how much reality is contained in their rhetoric of being friends of all the people.

Second, government needs to be much more inventive in extending the input of its citizens in government policy making. Everyone wanting a voice in policy making does not necessarily have good answers to all policy questions. But everybody has a right at least to a voice, to prove that the president, the governor, or the Senate is wrong. Had it not been for some of those "noisy, irksome students" in the mid-1960s, we might not have gotten out of the Vietnam war as soon as we did. Democracy rides upon the philosophy that the least of our fellow citizens has something to say. That principle should imply a great deal more consult-

5. For such a study of land-grant colleges in general see James Hightower, *Hard Tomatoes, Hard Times: The Failure of The Land-Grant College Complex* (Washington, D.C.: Agribusiness Accountability Project, 1972).

ing with the public about policy making than legislators find comfortable. The state house doors should be opened once in a while, not for a ceremonial hearing, but for a hearing to determine what the public wants. One of the travesties of the democratic process is that our "hearings" are mostly ceremony. Committee members never seriously expect to do anything different because of a hearing. This is treating the public like children. But children understand more than we sometimes assume, and they can be taught to understand even more through patient teaching. We need to lower the cost of information about public issues in time for citizens to help influence the decisions on those issues, and we need politicians who will assume the role of public educators.

Third, business people speak often about the importance of letting the market determine what they produce. But business has been inconsistent; it says that the customer is king, but it tries to tell the customer what he or she wants. One of the tests of that is the contempt with which the word *consumerism* is used by business people. For Adam Smith, the father of economic theory, consumerism could have been another name for a market-oriented economy. Are we really interested in paternalizing the public so that we produce those things *we* think it needs? If the public says it doesn't need a product or that a product doesn't work, is not business obliged to listen? In this sense we need more scientific intelligence in business. We need market research, not merely on what people will buy, but on what their experience teaches them to want.

Further, we should exploit the generalist and public roles of the churches in ways that will fulfill the promise of their charters. An Anglican prayer reads, "Bless all sorts and conditions of men." Although these days we are changing it to Bless all sorts and conditions of "people," the inclusion of the attribute of universality still makes a lot of theological and sociological sense. The churches collectively span as wide a spectrum of social groups in our society as any other institution, and church members represent a diversity of commitments that need to be built into public policy discussion. In this connection the church needs to wrestle with the practical implications of H. Richard Niebuhr's relational theory of value.[6] Niebuhr's essay "The Center of Value" continues to say more about what is wrong and what could be right about our society than any other ethical theory I have read. In that essay he dealt with the conflict between absolutism and relativism in values. An absolute value for one person is often a relative value for someone else. Nothing is more difficult in policy negotiations than trying to cut down to relative size those absolutisms that each of us brings into the discussion. The problem often surfaces in environmental policy questions. The value of a tree is one thing to a lumber company, another thing to squirrels, and still another thing to the atmospheric supply of oxygen. And the trick is for us to relate the value of the tree to humans but not deny or destroy its value to other entities that also have their claim upon that tree. By treating ourselves as the center of value or as the absolutistic determiners of value, we, in effect, make ourselves into God. In doing so, we add to the polytheism of a culture rather than living as part of a universal kingdom of value relations whose ruler is God. "You shall love all your neighbors as beings as valuable as yourself" might then be an "axiological" form of the great commandment.

The churches are called by their charter of faith to love God and all his creatures, which is the largest public service of all. As Margaret Mead said over ten years ago, church leaders of our time know that they live in a world too large to love. They find themselves reaching out to other institu-

6. H. Richard Niebuhr, *Radical Monotheism and Western Culture* (New York: Harper and Row, 1960), 100–13.

Epilogue: Malthusian Concern from 1800 to 1962

GERALD ALONZO SMITH

THE CONCERN for the environment and its resources that has been labeled Malthusian herein has gone by different names throughout its history. It has been classified under the headings of conservation, natural resource scarcity, environmental concern, and, more lately, ecology. Although Rachel Carson in 1962 aroused American public opinion to the dangers of abusing the environment, she was by no means the first to recognize the conflict between expanding industry and a delicate biotic and limited environment. Concern for the environment, which is derived from the realization that mankind is totally dependent for its existence upon the physical resources of this globe as well as on the proper functioning of many intricate reactions within the environment, has a long and widely based, if somewhat checkered, intellectual history.

Since the concern is over the scarcity of physical resources, both social scientists and physical scientists have a legitimate interest in it. But more precisely, the area of study wherein the physical sciences and the social sciences overlap will generate the knowledge that will aid in the resolution of how to utilize and allocate our natural resources. Accordingly, this essay is limited to physical scientists who took an intellectual interest in problems of scarcity and to social scientists who acknowledged that nonrenewable physical resources fulfilled a unique and essential need in society.

The significance of Thomas Robert Malthus' work was not in his solution to the problem of natural resource scarcity, but in the manner that he framed the problem.[1] Because Malthus discussed the dynamics of population growth and the limitations of the earth's resources, social scientists had to acknowledge that the problem of mankind's survival on a fixed, limited, and delicate environmental base was critical, particularly in view of the growing population and expanding industry.

In the debate between Malthus and his critics there was not much disagreement over the fundamental premise that he postulated. All the major social scientists accepted his belief that mankind's numbers would at some time in the future be determined by a limiting factor such as the "carrying capacity" of the earth. The controversial questions were: (1) When would this point in time be reached? and (2) Could mankind voluntarily and effectively limit its numbers and thus maintain a standard of living for the masses beyond a mere subsistence level?

As for the first question, the optimists believed that such a point in time was being pushed far into the future because of the improvements that man was experiencing during the Enlightment and Industrial Revolution. They argued that the world was underpopulated and that nothing stood in the way of an era of prosperity for all, except private ignorance and public inertia. It was in response to this view that Malthus published in 1798 his long pamphlet entitled *An*

1. Before Malthus, there were studies concerned with man's dependence upon the environment, but they were of a sporadic and tangential nature. See Charles E. Strangelend, *Pre-Malthusian Doctrines of Population: A Study in the History of Economic Theory* (New York: Columbia University Press, 1904); Joseph J. Spengler, *French Predecessors of Malthus* (Durham, N.C.: Duke University Press, 1942); and Clarence Glacken, *Traces on the Rhodian Shore: Nature and Culture in Western Thought from Ancient Times to the End of the Eighteenth Century* (Berkeley: University of California Press, 1976).

Essay on the Principle of Population, as It Affects the Future Improvement of Society; With Remarks on the Speculations of Mr. Godwin, M. Condorcet, and Other Writers. He took the position that overpopulation was a very serious and current problem and would not go away, as Godwin and others assumed. On the contrary, based as it was on indisputable physical laws of nature, overpopulation would always be a problem. Thus the intellectual battle lines were drawn and would continue unabated until the death of Malthus in 1834.[2]

The related question of whether mankind's numbers would increase so that the majority of the population would have to be satisfied with some subsistence level of existence or whether mankind would have the ability to control its numbers and thus maintain a higher standard of living for the masses was also actively debated during this time. Though Malthus himself did not put much faith in population control, several of his followers took a different view. Francis Place seems to have been the first to perceive the possibilities of birth control: "If, above all, it were once clearly understood, that it was not disreputable for married persons to avail themselves of such precautionary means as would, without being injurious to health, or destructive of female delicacy, prevent conception, a sufficient check might at once be given to the increase of population beyond the means of subsistence; vice and misery, to a prodigious extent, might be removed from society."[3]

John Stuart Mill accepted Place's conclusions and remained an active supporter of population control by means of education and state control. In his essay *On Liberty*, which has been acclaimed as one of the most brilliant de-

2. For a thorough investigation of the controversy between Malthus and his critics, see Kenneth Smith, *The Malthusian Controversy* (London: Routledge & Paul, 1951).

3. Francis Place, *Illustrations and Proofs of the Principle of Population*, as found in facsimile edition with notes by Norman E. Himes (London: George Allen & Unwin, 1930), 165.

fenses of the individual to think and act for himself, Mill wrote:

The fact itself, of causing the existence of a human being, is one of the most responsible actions in the range of human life. To undertake this responsibility—to bestow a life which may be either a curse or a blessing—unless the being on whom it is to be bestowed will have at least the ordinary chances of a desirable existence, is a crime against that being. And in a country either overpeopled, or threatened with being so, to produce children, beyond a very small number, with the effect of reducing the reward of labor by their competition, is a serious offense against all who live by the remuneration of their labor. The laws which, in many countries on the Continent, forbid marriage unless the parties can show that they have the means of supporting a family, do not exceed the legitimate powers of the State.[4]

In 1865 the economist William Stanley Jevons brought Malthusian thought into line with industrialization by stating that "the whole question turns upon the application of these [Malthusian] views to the consumption of coal. Our subsistence no longer depends upon our produce of corn. The momentous repeal of the Corn Laws throws us from corn upon coal."[5] Jevons wrote *The Coal Question* not so much to analyze natural resource scarcity problems as to probe into the source of the British industrial supremacy of his times. He prefaced his analysis with a summary statement of his principal hypothesis: "Renewed reflection has convinced me that my main position is only too strong and true. It is simply that we cannot long progress as we are now doing. I give the usual scientific reasons for supposing that coal must confer mighty influence and advantages upon its rich possessor, and I show that we now use much more of this invaluable aid than all other countries put together. But

4. John Stewart Mill, *On Liberty* (New York: Appleton-Century-Crofts, 1947), 110.
5. William Stanley Jevons, *The Coal Question: An Inquiry Concerning the Progress of the Nation, and the Probable Exhaustion of our Coal Mines*, ed. A. W. Flux (New York: A. M. Kelley, 1965), 195.

it is impossible that we should long maintain so singular a position."[6]

Jevons' position was quite straightforward. It was that British industry had taken advantage of the motive power of coal more than the industry of any other country had. Thus British industrial supremacy depended upon the use of vast amounts of coal. This supremacy could not last, however, because (1) the coal was becoming more difficult to obtain, and (2) other countries such as the United States and Germany had larger reserves of coal and were beginning to utilize their resources. More important, the economy of Great Britain would, in time, begin to stagnate. As the coal mines were exhausted, the British economy would slow down. For Jevons this would be a catastrophic event.[7] One gets the feeling that Jevons wrote his book more because of an exaggerated sense of nationalism, a major motif of the high Victorian age, than because of a fear of resource exhaustion. For example, when he discusses posterity, he clearly means British posterity only. His concern was how the British nation of the mid-nineteenth century should use its unparalled and never-to-be-repeated industrial greatness: "If we lavishly and boldly push forward in the creation of our riches, both material and intellectual, it is hard to over-estimate the pitch of beneficial influence to which we may attain in the present. But the maintenance of such a position is physically impossible. We have to make the momentous choice between brief but true greatness and longer continued mediocrity."[8]

At the same time Jevons was treating the importance of

6. *Ibid.*, xxx.
7. *Ibid.* Jevons was quite concerned about a slowdown in the economy, as shown in the two quotations in his frontispiece: "Non progredi est regredi" and "The progressive state is in reality the cheerful and the hearty state to all the different orders of society; the stationary is full, the declining melancholy" (Adam Smith).
8. *Ibid.*, 460.

coal to the British economy, an American, George Perkins Marsh, was undertaking a much more comprehensive project, a study of the impact of mankind upon nature. According to Marsh, through wanton destruction and profligate waste the earth was "fast becoming an unfit home for its noblest inhabitant, and another era of equal human crime and human improvidence . . . would reduce it to such a condition of impoverished productiveness, of shattered surface, of climactic excess, as to threaten the depravation, barbarism, and perhaps even extinction of the species."[9]

In many ways the studies of Jevons and Marsh complement each other. Jevons investigated the dependence of one country upon a particular resource at a particular time. Marsh investigated the impact of civilized man throughout history on his environment. Whereas Jevons' work was a scientific and detailed case study, Marsh's work was that of a generalist, as he himself recognized. He was concerned with the total biotic and land environment that supported civilization, not with the metals and fossil fuels that constructed and powered an industrial economy.

Marsh introduced his topic with a brief discussion that linked the fall of the ancient Roman Empire to a decrease in its natural resource base. Next, in a wide-ranging investigation, he generalized from the example of the Roman Empire to the whole of Western civilization. This section contains some of his most memorable indictments and expressions of concern over Western man's destruction of his environment. After this general introduction, he discussed man's role in plant and animal domestication and the effects of such domestication upon the organic and land environment. Next, in the largest chapter, entitled "The Woods," he explored the consequences of deforestation, which was one of his chief concerns. He had been personally involved in the deforestation on the Green Mountain

9. George Perkins Marsh, *Man and Nature*, ed. David Lowenthal (Cambridge, Mass.: Harvard University Press, 1965), 43.

slopes of his native Vermont, and he had observed the scrub and desert regions of the Mediterranean. The remainder of the book surveyed man's impact upon two other aspects of nature, water and dunes. He concluded by showing that man's actions, though individually negligible, may in the aggregate alter the structure, composition, and destiny of the earth and its inhabitants.

Marsh's analysis attracted wide attention at the time. It directly inspired, in 1873, a concerned statement by the American Association for the Advancement of Science that led Congress to establish the Division of Forestry in 1882 and to set aside certain lands as forest preserves. From this forestry division came the leaders of the conservation movement that spread over the United States from 1890 to 1910. Among these leaders was B. E. Fernow, who, in 1886, took charge of forestry work in the United States Department of Agriculture. The forester Gifford Pinchot also played a leading role in the movement.

The foresters were concerned with the indiscriminate deforestation taking place in the United States. By 1890 the American frontier was coming to an end. Americans in search of their manifest destiny could no longer face west and see unlimited expanses of forest resources beckoning to them. It was the end of an era, and it is no surprise that, at this critical time in its history, the United States stopped momentarily to take a rough inventory of its natural resources and to consider just how such resources should be utilized. The forests were the first of the great natural resources in the United States to be depleted rapidly and wantonly enough to attract attention and cause alarm.[10]

The Geological Survey of Pennsylvania showed a concern over oil supplies as early as 1874. In 1883 the Pennsyl-

10. Samuel Hays, *Conservation and the Gospel of Efficiency* (Cambridge, Mass.: Harvard University Press, 1959); John Ise, *The United States Forest Policy* (New Haven, Conn.: Yale University Press, 1920); or M. Nelson McGreary, *Gifford Pinchot, Forester/Politician* (Princeton, N.J.: Princeton University Press, 1960), Pt. 1, pp. 19–210.

vania state geologist, Peter Lesley, sounded a distinctly warning note: "The next generation will gather from our oil history, with angry astonishment, a lesson of warning in political economy, only useless because coming too late."[11]

Nathaniel Southgate Shaler, professor of geology at Harvard, expressed a conservationist philosophy similar to that of Marsh, but he emphasized the importance of minerals and the fertility of the soil. In "The Economic Aspects of Soil Erosion" Shaler warned his readers in vigorous language that their fertile soil resource would wash away if American farmers continued to abuse the land.[12] This warning would ring true to the many American farmers who saw their topsoil either wash away or blow away during the Dust Bowl era. In the preface of his best-known book, *Man and the Earth,* Shaler noted: "As a teacher of Geology, I have seen that there is a complete lack of understanding in our communities as to the duty we owe to our successors in their use of these limited resources."[13]

It is important to note that Shaler, like Marsh, recognized that the careful conservation of America's resources would not only require more information derived from careful research, but, more essential, a change in American attitude. More was needed than the optimistic utilitarian approach that progress would be able to resolve all the problems of resource scarcity. There was a need for a change in heart, for a love of the earth and a respect for posterity. Shaler concluded *Man and the Earth* with this exhortation:

The great gain we are to have from the modern knowledge of the world is in the change of attitude it is to bring about: in the sense of kinship with the anciently alien realm and of duty by the great inheritance of life. To the making of this new spirit no great body

11. John Ise, *The United States Oil Policy* (New Haven, Conn.: Yale University Press, 1926), 275.

12. Nathaniel Southgate Shaler, "The Economic Aspects of Soil Erosion," *National Geographic Magazine,* VII (1896), 328–377.

13. Nathaniel Southgate Shaler, *Man and the Earth* (New York: Fox, Duffield, 1905), i.

of learning needs go; it will depend for its development far more on the way of approach than on the mass of the knowledge that is gained. So soon as men come to feel themselves as really the children of the world, the tides of affection that instinctively tend toward it, but have been sorely hindered by ancient misunderstandings, will help in the good work, and give us souls reconciled to their great house and eager to help its order.[14]

Charles Van Hise, professor of geology at the University of Wisconsin, also played a vital role in the conservation movement. His book *The Conservation of Natural Resources in the United States*, first published in 1910, became the textbook most often used in conservation courses in the universities. It was illustrated, factual, and straightforward in its message to Americans to stop wasting their fossil fuels, water, forests, and land.

At the height of the conservation movement, about 1910, some economists took up the challenge to incorporate natural resources into the scope of economic analysis and began to explore the appropriate rate of utilization of natural resources by society.[15] Were such natural resources to be treated by economists in the same way as all other factors of production (that is, as a portion of society's homogenous capital) or were they somehow unique and, therefore, in need of special consideration? Most economists did not (and do not) think that natural resources were unique factors of production but that they were similar to other factors and did not warrant special treatment in their analysis.

The conservation movement directly rejected this method of analysis, used by orthodox economists. The conservationist claimed, not only that natural resources were unique, but that mankind had a moral duty to preserve for future generations the vital resources as nearly unimpaired as the nature of the case admits. H. J. Davenport, an econ-

14. *Ibid.*, 232–33.

15. B. F. Fernow, "The Providential Functions of Government with Special Reference to Natural Resources," *American Association for the Advancement of Sciences, Proceedings*, XLIV (1895), 344.

omist at the University of Chicago, went to the heart of the argument between economist and conservationist regarding natural resources and capital in the following selection written in 1911.

I should like after all to give to this discussion its essential theoretical significance. We economists have not rightly analyzed the notion of capital. We have failed to see that some of the capital is as iniquituous as other of the capital is beneficent. Noting that some of it was good, we have inferred that all of it is good. By our bad analysis, in our blindness to the distinction between social productivity and private productivity, between that which ethically is production and that which ethically is predation, we have stood as defenders of all. . . .

There needs, it seems, that some theoretical muckraking be done. The ostrich method of curing ills is foredoomed to failure.[16]

Most economists were unwilling to follow Davenport's suggestion and to admit of ethical distinctions between capital that resulted from legitimate productive activities and capital that resulted from acts of predation, such as depleting the fertility of the soil, exhausting the forests, and polluting water resources. There are two reasons for this aversion to making such a distinction. First, because ethical criteria cannot be measured, they are difficult to deal with in a tightly organized and quantifiable model, which seems to be the immediate and final goal of much economic analysis. Second, if ethical criteria are admitted into a model, accusations of sentimentalism and emotionalism can be directed toward its creator.

Some economists, however, did attempt an analysis of the economic implications of natural resource utilization. At the University of Wisconsin, Richard T. Ely and Lewis C. Gray led the way, as they explored various facets of the relationship between economic theory and natural re-

16. H. J. Davenport, "The Extent and Significance of the Unearned Increment," *Papers and Discussions of the American Economic Association*, I (1911), 322–33.

sources. Gray's remarkable pioneer study, "Economic Possibilities of Conservation," appeared in 1913. He showed more insight than many later economists when he stated that "the real heart of the conservation problem presents an issue which taxes the resources of economic theory to the utmost. This issue is the problem of adjusting the conflict between the interest of the present and the future."[17]

Having begun his study by distinguishing between renewable and nonrenewable resources, Gray scientifically delineated the economic possibilities of conservation with regard to nonrenewable resources. First, he investigated the criterion of present value maximization, which is the criterion that almost all later economists have used to determine the optimal rate of utilization on nonrenewable resources.[18] Though Gray was thoroughly familiar with the present value maximization criterion, he was quite aware that such a criterion would not aid in achieving the goals of the conservation movement. His familiarity with the criterion was apparent in his illustration of the importance of interest rates, the finiteness of the resource, and future price expectations in the present value maximization mode. This familiarity was even more evident in an article he published a year later.[19] This recognition of the limits of the present value maximization criterion regarding the conservation

17. Lewis C. Gray, "Economic Possibilities of Conservation," *Quarterly Journal of Economics*, XXVII (1913), 499.

18. The present value maximization criterion discounts all monetary benefits from a future stream of natural resources to their present value and then maximizes this present value. The mathematical formulas are as follows: For discrete time periods, maximize present value where

$$\text{Present Value} = \sum_{t=1}^{N} \frac{B_t}{(1 + i)^t} \qquad \begin{aligned} \text{where } t &= \text{time} \\ B_t &= \text{benefits in time } t \\ i &= \text{discount rate} \end{aligned}$$

For continuous time periods,

$$\text{Present Value} = \int_{0}^{N} e^{-it}(B_t)dt$$

19. Lewis C. Gray, "Rent under the Assumption of Exhaustibility," *Quarterly Journal of Economics*, XXVIII (1914), 466–89.

goal is something that apparently no other economist down to the time of Talbot Page had explicitly noticed. In 1977 Page described the relationship in the following manner: "It is no more appropriate to conclude that the sustainable yield criterion [the conservation criterion] is invalid because it does not satisfy the present value criterion than it is appropriate to conclude that the present value criterion is invalid because it does not satisfy the sustainable yield criterion. One cannot use one criterion to bludgeon another. They are on the same logical level . . . they imply different states of the world."[20]

This awareness of the two contrary goals—the present value maximization goal and the conservation goal—prompted Gray to ask the crucial question, "Where is the proper balance between utilization [present value maximization] and conservation?" Having considered several contrary responses to this question, he stated, first, that "utilization must not be so restricted as either to impair the treasured result of past progress or to handicap seriously the rate of progress in the future." Next, he wondered if a rapid and exploitative rate of utilization of resources is necessary for such progress in the future. He then worked himself out of his apparent inconsistency by his discerning definition of progress:

Exploitation results in maximum production under certain conditions, but maximum production does not necessarily mean progress. . . . Maximum production may be accompanied by a manner of life which is not consistent with the highest social development. . . . A vast amount of consumption is neither based on welfare, nor on enjoyment; it is solely dictated by convention. The enormous waste of coal required for the electrical advertising in our great cities is illustrative of this exploitative consumption. As Professor H. J. Davenport has expressed it, "Every great white way in every American city is nightly one more chemical orgy of waste, a crime of competitive advertising for which some day

20. Talbot Page, *Conservation and Economic Efficiency* (Baltimore: Johns Hopkins Press, 1977), 188.

thousands of individuals must shiver for months." The necessities of conservation may compel the economist to enlarge his field so as to apply the test of economy as one of the criteria for the justification of wants.[21]

Unfortunately mainstream economic theory has not heeded Gray's prophetic call to enlarge its field "so as to apply the test of economy as one of the criteria for the justification of wants." Instead it has quite simplistically and rather arrogantly assumed that all effective wants are equally justified, a position that can only lead to exploitation of not only natural resources but human resources as well. Such exploitation is the complete opposite of economy in any conservationist (or historical) sense. Neglect of such a distinction explains the confusion that often arises in the mind of a conservationist when it appears that economic theory is noneconomic. Also this equal justification of wants is probably one of the reasons why the conventional economic theorist has been so attracted to the present value maximization criterion. Since such a criterion sets the value of everything, including the discount rate, strictly from the known wants of the present generation, the really difficult and important question of what to do about absolute biophysical shortages can be ignored, as well as the consequent normative problem of deciding between present luxuries and future vital needs.

In many ways this pioneering effort of Gray reached a level of sophistication and breadth of understanding in combining economic theory and conservation principles that was not to be reached again for many years. It would be decades before economists would realize that present value maximization criteria would not guarantee the welfare of future generations. Gray instinctively grasped what recently Talbot Page and James Doilney have laboriously proved, that present value maximization analysis is one thing and

21. Gray, "Economic Possibilities of Conservation," 516.

conservation is another thing and that both ethical standards have to be considered when making societal decisions. [22] As Gray phrased it, "Philosophically considered, the question of present value maximum utilization or careful conservation of resources cannot be answered with finality without such a definite comprehension of the purpose of human existence as has not been vouchsafed the race. In the absence of more infallible foundations we shall doubtless lean on the 'crutch of common sense.'"[23] Unfortunately some economists thought that they could do without the "crutch of common sense" and went flying off into the higher mathematics of present value maximization models to resolve this issue. After some forty years, it is becoming clearer that although one's academic reputation can soar in the rarefied air of higher mathematical models, the reality of human existence takes place on or close to the surface of this globe. And because of the inherently infinite complexities of many of the problems of allocating resources to meet the needs of the global populace, we should always utilize the "crutch of common sense" in all our decisions.

Richard T. Ely was Lewis C. Gray's professor at the University of Wisconsin; consequently, it is difficult to determine whose ideas should take precedence in time. Ely takes a quite different approach to the problem of conservation than does Gray. He assumes very categorically that conservation of certain resources is the right approach and, hence, that indispensable natural resources are in a class by themselves and that the interest rate should have no influence on their rate of utilization. [24] This implicitly eliminates any present value maximization method of proceeding and, as

22. Page, *Conservation and Economic Efficiency,* 250; James Doilney, "Equity, Efficiency, and Intertemporal Resource Allocation Decisions" (Ph.D. dissertation, University of Maryland, 1974), Chap. III, p. 13.

23. Gray, "Economic Possibilities of Conservation," 515.

24. Richard T. Ely, "Conservation and Economic Theory," in Richard T. Ely (ed.), *The Foundation of National Prosperity: Studies In the Conservation of Permanent National Resources* (New York: MacMillan, 1917), 36.

such, makes Ely's approach quite distinct from that of most economists who have investigated the problem of optimal rate of utilization of natural resources.

Ely was able to come to such a conclusion because of his training in the German historical school, or inductive method of political economy. As Ely acknowledged in his essay, his analysis of the rate of utilization of resources owed much to the German economist Freiderich List. Although List's *National System of Political Economy* dealt primarily with the development of productive capacity through appropriate tariff policies, Ely showed that List's theory of productive powers is easily and naturally applied to the conservation of vital resources. Though List acknowledges the need for present productivity, he regards as more important the development of productive powers for the future. Since one of the main premises of the conservation ethic is that society should have a careful regard for productive powers in the future, Ely was easily able to show, through List's analysis, the necessity of conservation policies. Ely concluded that laissez-faire economic policies would not ensure appropriate conservation of vital resources and that some public ownership or regulation or both would be necessary if such resources were to be preserved.

Though a few other economists were interested in the study of economic theory as it applied to the conservation of natural resources, their work was somewhat tangential to the main issue. Such was the work of Thomas N. Carver, an economist at Harvard who was mainly interested in human resources, and Ralph Hess, an economist at the University of Wisconsin.[25]

As the conservation movement lost much of its popular support during and after World War I, the few economists who had attempted a synthesis of economic theory and conservation principles apparently lost their interest in continu-

25. Thomas N. Carver, "Conservation of Human Resources," 275–361, and Ralph Hess, "Conservation and Economic Evolution" 95–187, both *ibid.*

ing this line of research. It is interesting to note that they seemed to shift their interest to the newly developing sub-discipline of agricultural economics. For instance, Ely became editor of *Land Economics* and collaborated on a much-used textbook of the same name while doing his research on taxation of land resources. Gray became president of the fledgling American Farm Economic Association, author of a classic two-volume history of southern agriculture, and later an active administrator in the Land Resettlement Division of the Department of Agriculture during the New Deal era.

The intellectual void that remained when Ely, Gray, and others turned their attention away from the analysis of optimal natural resource utilization was filled by one indomitable academic. John Ise was born in 1885, very close to the geographical center of the United States. After graduate studies at Harvard, he returned to the University of Kansas where he wrote three major books—*The U.S. Forest Policy* (1920), *The U.S. Oil Policy* (1927), and *The U.S. National Parks* (1961)—and an outstanding monograph in the *American Economic Review*, "The Theory of Value as Applied to Natural Resources" (1925). Although Ise understood and appreciated the frontier ethic with regard to natural resources, he also saw that, in the long run, it was destructive to the American way of life. In his first book he wrote:

The history of the United States is fundamentally a history of rapid exploitation of immensely valuable natural resources. The possession and exploitation of these resources have given most of the distinctive traits to American character, economic development, and even political and social institutions. Whatever preeminence the United States may have among the nations of the world, in industrial activity, efficiency and enterprise, in standards of comfort in living, in wealth, and even in such social and educational institutions as are dependent upon great wealth, must be attributed to the possession of these great natural resources; and the maintenance of our preeminence in these respects is dependent upon a wise and economical use of remaining resources. Thus the question of conservation is one of the most important questions before the American people, and if the present study throws even a weak and flickering light upon that question, its publication will be abundantly justified. [26]

Ise's *The U.S. Oil Policy* is a socioeconomic classic, much ahead of its time. His discussion of the social costs and benefits of the automobile age is contemporary today. His premonition that on the international scene "there are many reasons for believing that oil will never be left entirely to unfettered economic sale and purchase" has turned out to be only too true in our time. [27]

Ise also spent a large amount of his time investigating the alleged benefits that society receives from a rapid exploitation of natural resources. Unlike most economists, he was willing to ask critical questions of much of the consumption of his age:

Can we say, categorically, that the pleasure of riding from nowhere to nowhere at 80 miles an hour is inferior in quality to the pleasure of listening to the *Eroica* symphony or the Gotterdammerung? As economists, we have always evaded such questions. We have assumed that whatever the people want has economic utility whether bootleg gin or Beethoven, and from the predominance of demand for the former have assumed that American happiness was increasing day by day in every way. . . .

Perhaps much of our traditional economics is pointless and of little avail, a foundation with no superstructure, a prologue without the opera. The production of goods, more goods, more things, mountain of things—to what purpose? [28]

In his remarkable monograph "The Theory of Value as Applied to Natural Resources," Ise set himself to the crucial task of determining the appropriate pricing policy for

26. Ise, *The United States Forest Policy*, preface.
27. Ise, *The United States Oil Policy*, 173.
28. John Ise, *The American Way* (Lawrence, Kan.: Allan Press, 1955), 34.

America's natural resources. To do this he distinguished between resources assumed to have substitutes and resources assumed to have no substitutes. For resources having no substitutes, either for themselves or for their products, the question was asked, "How much difference are we justified in making between present wants and future wants?" Ise concluded, as Gray had, that it is impossible to answer this question definitely or precisely: "Doubtless future wants should be discounted somewhat, because of various contingencies and uncertainities, but it is doubtful if the wants of the next generation, for instance, should be rated less than half as important as our own. This would mean a discount of about two per cent a year."[29]

Ise's main contribution to the price theory of natural resources was in the largest and most important category, resources with available substitutes. "But for some of these resources, and for some of the hundreds of products made from them, substitutes will be available. On the theory of forthcoming substitutes, where should prices be fixed? The answer here is clear. Prices of the resources, or of the products derived from these resources, should be fixed at a point approximating the cost of producing adequate and satisfactory substitutes."[30]

Pricing nonrenewable resources at the same level as the cost of producing adequate and satisfactory substitutes would have two desirable consequences, according to Ise. First, it would conserve our exhaustible resources; second, it would stimulate efforts to find a variety of adequate substitutes from renewable resources. Unfortunately, Ise was unaware of the work of Frederick Soddy, an English chemist and heretical economist who was shocked by economists' lack of attention to the physical coordinates of value and

29. John Ise, "The Theory of Value as Applied to Natural Resources," *American Economic Review*, XV (June, 1925), 285.
30. *Ibid.*, 286.

urged them to pay attention to the principles of thermodynamics. Soddy's analysis would have provided a firm
biophysical, if not metaphysical, basis for many of the
exhortations of Ise.

John Ise was a lone voice crying in the darkness of economic theory. There was no follow-up on this article. Instead, the economic theorists followed the lead of Harold
Hotelling, who, in a 1931 article entitled "The Economics
of Exhaustible Resources," attempted to discover what
maximizes the present value of the stream of consumer benefits from the stock of natural resources.[31] Because the
market encourages firms to maximize the present value of
their profit stream, even with exhaustible resources, Hotelling wondered whether market forces would maximize the
present value of consumer benefits. He found that under
competitive conditions the market tends to lead toward
present value maximization of consumer benefits. It is important to note that Hotelling was working under the assumption that new resources can always be found or that
technology will come up with suitable substitutes for the
vital natural resources. In other words, there is no such
thing as absolute shortage or even the possibility of absolute
shortage, in his world view. For the most part, the economics profession has followed Hotelling's line of analysis and
has explicitly or implicitly assumed that, for any rate of
utilization of natural resources, what is optimal for the consumption of the present generation will also be optimal for
the consumption of future generations. As a result, most
economists have felt that no unique effort should be made
in the conservation of any of our natural resources. Page
and Doilney, however, have recently shown that present
value maximization, if used as society's only rate of utiliza-

---

31. Harold Hotelling, "The Economics of Exhaustable Resources," *Journal
of Political Economy*, XXXIX (1931), 137–75.

tion of natural resources, can lead to disastrously low future welfare levels.[32] Accordingly, I shall not attempt to outline the body of literature that has derived its inspiration from Hotelling's methodology. Those writings may be useful in resolving certain problems, but with their assumption of un-limited natural resources or the ability of technology to pro-vide such resources, they do not belong in a history of the Malthusian or conservation tradition. I have mentioned them merely to show where conservation principles were ambushed in the history of economic thought.

During the 1930s intellectual concern for the conserva-tion of natural resources dimmed somewhat. Four causes are apparently responsible for this decline. First, the socio-economic problems of the Depression took precedence over all other problems. Second, American education had become more specialized and departmentalized. Scientists were coming to know more about less. The problem of wisely allocating natural resources requires a broad under-standing of many areas of science such as geology, physics, ethics, economics. Third, the social sciences were becom-ing more positivistic in their methodology.[33] Because the is-sues involved in the conservation of resources quickly lead to normative judgements, the social scientists became more reluctant to deal with such issues. Fourth, there was a rising faith that technology would resolve the problems of natural resource scarcity and that conservation was not really needed.

What concern there was over natural resources focused upon a problem that was only too apparent during the Dust Bowl era, the depletion of fertile topsoil through both water and wind erosion. As the geographer Carl O. Sauer ex-pressed it in the 1930s, "Soil destruction is the most wide-

32. Page, *Conservation and Economic Efficiency*, 250; Doilney, "Equity, Efficiency, and Intertemporal Resource Allocation Decisions," 111–13.

33. The classic expression of this attitude in the field of economics is Lionel Robbins, *An Essay on the Nature and Significance of Economic Science* (Lon-don: MacMillan, 1932).

spread and most serious debit to be entered against colonial commercial exploitation."[34]

After a description of such soil destruction, Sauer rejected the view that technology would resolve the food problems of the world: "The easy denial of our dilemma by referring it to the technologist is in large measure wishful thinking." According to Sauer, society still has to resolve the question of how to conserve natural resources, a problem that Americans have not faced squarely. "The doctrine of a passing frontier of nature replaced by a permanently and sufficiently expanding frontier of technology is a contemporary and characteristic expression of occidental culture, itself a historical-geographic product. This 'frontier' attitude has the recklessness of an optimism that has become habitual, but which is residual from the brave days when north-European freebooters overran the world and put it under tribute. We have not yet learned the difference between yield and loot. We do not like to be economic realists."[35]

During World War II, enormous quantities of resources were used up, and shortly after the war there were some misgivings about the adequacy of the United States resource base to meet the greatly increased and steadily increasing demands for raw materials. This concern led to the establishment of the president's Materials Policy Commission in 1951 and to its successor, the Resources for the Future organization. This commission, now usually called the Paley Commission, concluded that the period of unlimited resource availability was over for the United States; nevertheless, scarce resources could be obtained by increased foreign trade and the resource base could be expanded by new technology.

Not all Americans accepted this guardedly optimistic

34. Carl O. Sauer, "Theme of Plant and Animal Destruction in Economic History," *Journal of Farm Economics*, XX (1938) 765–76. Reprinted in John Leighly (ed.), *Land and Life* (Berkeley: University of California Press, 1963), 151.

35. *Ibid.*, 154.

conclusion that natural resources were plentiful. In a response to the Paley Commission, Samuel Ordway states, "It does not seem likely that imports or 'technology' will be the means of keeping us from ultimately reaching the limit of growth."[36]

However, in the hubris of the post-World War II years the belief that the depletion of resources was the most serious problem facing the United States was held by only a small minority of scholars. During this Cold War era, urged on by competition with the Soviet Union, most social scientists saw the problem to be the opposite, that is, how we could move our economy to grow ever more rapidly and use even more resources. Because of their faith in technology such scientists disregarded any warnings of absolute shortages or environmental disruption. It would not be until Rachel Carson wrote the *Silent Spring* in 1962 that once again a large number of Americans gradually began to concern themselves with the depletion of resources and corresponding abuse of the environment upon which their very life and society depend.[37]

36. Samuel Ordway, "Possible Limits of Raw-Material Consumption," in William L. Thomas, Jr. (ed.), *Man's Role in Changing the Face of the Earth* (Chicago: University of Chicago Press, 1956), 994.

37. For a detailed historical study of the personalities and ideas that dominated the Conservation movement after 1962, see Donald Fleming, "Roots of the New Conservation Movement," *Perspectives in American History*, VI (1972), 7–91.

Notes on Contributors

Kenneth E. Boulding is a distinguished economist, systems theorist, and social scientist, who is widely published and acclaimed as one of our century's seminal thinkers in fields of human system organization and behavior. He is on the faculty of the University of Colorado, has served as president of the American Economic Association and is president of the American Association for the Advancement of Science.

Garrett Hardin is a scientist of the first order whose discipline, human ecology, intersects many others. His books and essays are considered standard texts in the study of population, resources, and environmental issues. A founder of the Environmental Fund and Zero Population Growth, he is internationally recognized for his contributions to the study of environmental impacts of social policy. Hardin is professor of human ecology at the University of California at Santa Barbara.

Herman E. Daly is an economist who represents the tradition of steady-state economics and is noted for his critique of uncritical, growth-oriented economic systems. He is professor of economics at Louisiana State University and an author widely read not only by those in his field but by environmentalists, theologians, and ethicists. Daly's contributions outside the university are as significant as his scholarly work. He is a regular consultant to various government agencies, to the National Council of Churches, and to the World Council of Churches.

Robert F. Chandler is an agronomist by training and choice and is recognized for his administrative ability as president of the University of New Hampshire. He was chosen by the Rockefeller

Foundation to organize and direct the International Rice Research Institute in the Philippines. Upon retirement from that post he organized and directed the Asian Vegetable Research and Training Center in Taiwan. Chandler's work enabled "the green revolution."

Harmon L. Smith, Jr., is a moral theologian and ethicist of international note and is widely published in fields of medical ethics and Christian social ethics. Smith fulfills a joint appointment at Duke University as professor of moral theology in the Divinity School and professor of community medicine in the Medical Center. An Episcopal priest, Smith brings together in his person and profession the often competitive elements of religion and the scientific and technical dimensions of life in the contemporary university.

John C. Bennett is president emeritus of Union Theological Seminary in New York City and professor of Christian ethics at Claremont School of Theology in California. His scholarly work in political ethics and social morality spans three decades; and his work with the National Council of Churches and World Council of Churches has catapulted him into the forefront of controversy throughout his career, a position he has occupied with characteristic grace and scholarly acumen.

Donald W. Shriver, Jr., is president of Union Theological Seminary in New York City, a Presbyterian minister of Virginia origins, and an urbane critic of contemporary urban society. An author of pastoral and technical articles on social ethics and books on sociological ethics, he is an interdisciplinarian skilled in the integration of the humanities, technologies, and social sciences both in academe and nonacademic society. Shriver represents the perspective of the "generalist" in the university, the church, and society.

Gerald Alonzo Smith is a coeditor of this volume, research associate with the Project on Science and Social Policy, and a Ph.D. candidate in economics at Louisiana State University. He holds advanced degrees in history, theology, agronomy, and economics—a background conducive to his examination of humanity's fundamental structural relationship to the world.

William M. Finnin, Jr. is coeditor of this volume, director of the Project on Science and Social Policy, and campus minister for United Methodists and Presbyterians at The Uniting Campus Ministry at Louisiana State University. He is an Underwood Fellow of the Danforth Foundation and a doctoral student in social ethics at the Iliff School of Theology in Colorado.

Index

DATE DUE